ONE THING AT A TIME

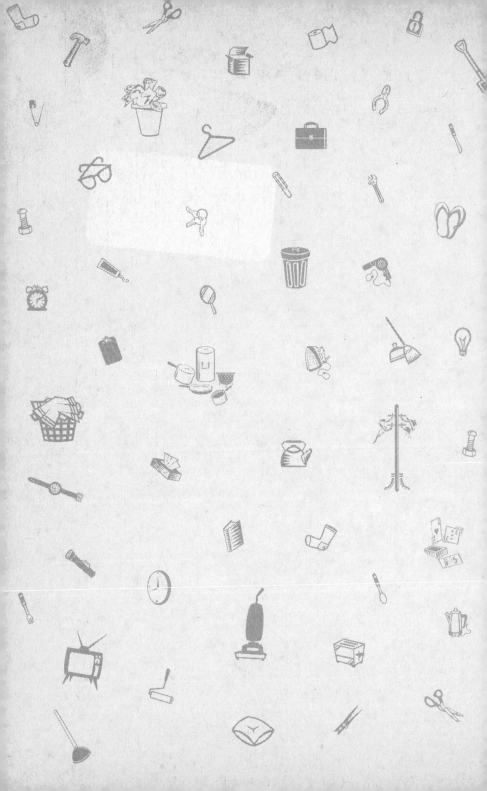

ALSO BY CINDY GLOVINSKY

Making Peace with the Things in Your Life

ONE THING AT A TIME

100 SIMPLE WAYS

TO LIVE CLUTTER-FREE EVERY DAY

CINDY GLOVINSKY, M.S.W., A.C.S.W.

ST. MARTIN'S GRIFFIN ♏ NEW YORK

www.stmartins.com

ISBN 0-312-32486-3
EAN 978-0312-32486-5

Book Design by Gretchen Achilles

FIRST EDITION: JULY 2004

10 9 8 7 6 5 4 3 2 1

The ordinary arts we practice every day at home
are of more importance to the soul than their
simplicity might suggest.

—THOMAS MOORE

CONTENTS

ACKNOWLEDGMENTS

This book was written immediately after I attended the conferences of two extraordinary organizations: the National Study Group on Chronic Disorganization and the National Association of Professional Organizers. Its contents were influenced in multiple ways by conversations and seminars during these conferences. A number of individuals from the organizations provided specific suggestions and/or editorial help, including Sheila Delson, Sara Bassett, Terry Prince, Debbie Stanley, Yanique Redwood-Jones, and Jill Lawrence. I want to thank all of these people for their support, not only in producing this book, but in countless other ways.

I'm also grateful to my agent, Andrea Pedolsky, for helping me to conceptualize the book proposal, and to my editor, Marian Lizzi, for her enthusiasm and superior craftsmanship. Additional thanks to all other staff members at St. Martin's Press who helped to produce and distribute the book.

Without the right supports, I would not have been able to write this book, and I thank all my friends and family just for being there. Special thanks to my Sunday morning writing group and to Matthew Ferguson, Marni Glovinsky, Bob Addison, Lafe Harter, Charlotte Harter, Jeanetta Housh, Amy Pershing, and, most of all, to my husband, Ira, for his love and support during this challenging time. Finally, thanks to my organizing and therapy clients, from whom I continue to learn new things every day about living clutter-free.

ONE THING AT A TIME

INTRODUCTION

You can't believe it, but they're back. Once again, piles of papers, books, clothes, and other material Things are camping all over your living space like a pack of tiresome relatives, camouflaging your furniture and clogging up your life. This despite the fact that not long ago you celebrated the successful conclusion of weeks of marathon de-cluttering and organizing. You were so certain that you'd finally resolved the issue of Things once and for all that you called in an interior designer and redecorated the whole place.

And now they're back.

What's the use? you think. Why try to get rid of clutter when the piles always come back anyway?

If clutter keeps coming back no matter what you do, take heart. This book will help you to keep the piles from reaccumulating so you can live more clutter-free *every* day, not just the day after you've de-cluttered. The 100 ideas presented here were designed not merely to get rid of clutter but also to keep it from cropping up in the first place. Once you're able to keep clutter from piling up at all, you'll never again have to experience the drudgery of long-term de-cluttering. Although at times you might still choose to let small piles accumulate while you focus on living, cycles of clutter that take days, weeks, or even months to remove will be a thing of the past. No more *big* clutter ever again.

Most books on dealing with this problem focus exclusively on de-cluttering and organizing. They might enable you to create a well-organized environment, but they don't tell you how to keep it that way. This book will help you to establish a permanently clutter-free way of life. Believe it or not, this will not require enormous effort on your part—just small adjustments here and there to your current thoughts, habits, and surroundings. Once you've gotten rid of the bulk of your clutter, maintenance is a matter of tweaking. And if you're still in the de-cluttering phase, starting maintenance *now* with the help of these 100 suggestions will protect you from backsliding when you've finished. While our primary focus is on maintenance, much of the material here is also relevant to de-cluttering.

In my previous book, *Making Peace with the Things in Your Life,* I explored the causes of chronic disorganization—defined as clutter that is "perpetual, long lasting, and resistant to change"—and described a step-by-step program of lifestyle change, with an emphasis on de-cluttering. That book was about revolutionary change; this book is about daily maintenance and prevention. While *Making Peace* presented a systematic program, *One Thing at a Time* offers a smorgasbord of individual ideas that can be combined as you like, resulting in less and less clutter intruding on your daily life. It is meant to be both a companion to the earlier book and an alternative for readers who prefer a less linear approach.

As a professional organizer who has helped hundreds of clients to free themselves from ongoing clutter, I've come to believe that to live free of big clutter, you need to:

- set up a user-friendly environment

- use positive self-talk

- replace clutter-creating habits with clutter-reducing habits

- use proactive strategies and tools

- enlist the help of others

- practice self-care

All of the ideas in this book stem from this list. **Setting up a user-friendly environment** isn't essential for keeping clutter at a minimum, but it makes it a lot easier. To be user-friendly, your space needs to be free of excess items. Thus, part of maintenance is routine purging. Homes for items need to be conveniently located, easy to find, and as visible as possible. The practical suggestions in this book will help you to make your household user-friendly.

What you say to yourself about your possessions can make the difference between clutter-bound and clutter-free living. Most chronically disorganized people have been blamed and shamed over their difficulties, and their heads are filled with negative tapes that make them want to avoid the whole issue. Some of the ideas in this book take the form of statements that counter these negative thoughts with **positive self-talk**. Other statements and questions help to reshape your thinking about critical aspects of organizing. To help internalize a statement or question, copy it twenty times a day for a week, write it on a sign and tape it to your mirror, or repeat it over and over on tape and replay it as you meditate or go to sleep.

While changing what you say to yourself is important, if you want to live clutter-free, you must also change what you *do*. In other words, you need to establish the right habits. A number of the ideas in this book are designed to help you painlessly **replace clutter-creating habits with clutter-reducing habits**. In working to establish new habits, be patient with yourself. Changing habits takes a long time for most of us, and emotional resistance may make it take even longer. But every clutter-reducing habit you're able to firmly establish will make the piles a little smaller.

To shrink the piles even more, you need to strategize. Instead of simply reacting to circumstances, you'll learn here how to deal with your possessions by **using proactive strategies** including systematic scanning, making checklists, declaring special days, and breaking down big tasks into small ones. You'll also need to **make use of the right tools**. Even a simple tool such as a clipboard or a letter opener can help eliminate clutter, and a number of the ideas here involve the use of tools.

Enlisting the help of others can make the difference between more clutter and less clutter in your life. Some people may currently be making more clutter in your space, and in such cases "enlisting help" means persuading them to stop. At the same time, you may want to actively recruit an individual or group that can help support your efforts at clutter-free living. Some suggestions focus on enlisting help.

Finally, living clutter-free requires that you take care of yourself. Things have a way of piling up when you don't feel energetic and happy. Certain aspects of **self-care**—going to bed earlier, getting enough exercise, fresh air, and sunlight, even grooming and wardrobe—are particularly relevant to the clutter-free lifestyle, and some of my ideas simply encourage you to take care of yourself.

Not every idea in this book will feel appropriate for you, and you don't need to make use of them all for the level of daily clutter to go down significantly. Choose what will work for you and ignore the rest. The ideas here are by no means exhaustive, and my hope is that other ideas along similar lines will occur to you as you begin to work with them. The more such ideas you put into effect, the less clutter will continue to occupy your life.

The best way to work with these ideas is *one at a time*. To help you focus on one idea at a time, I've deliberately refrained from grouping the suggestions into categories. Before you start working with individual ideas, skim through the whole book, highlighting those concepts that you feel will help you the most. Then look back through the highlighted ideas and choose one that you think will be easy for you to put into effect. For one week, focus on this one idea as if your life depended on it and forget about all the others. To you, it's the only idea in the world. If you're a natural multitasker, this might feel unnatural at first, but give it a chance anyway and see if it becomes more comfortable over time. If it doesn't, you can always shift to an approach that better suits your personal style.

Once you've settled on an idea in this book, do whatever you need to do in order to put it into action. If you need to buy equipment, put up a sign, or mark something in your calendar, do so. If the idea is a statement that requires repetition, copy or record it as described above. If it's a daily habit, practice the new habit for at least three days before you move on to the next suggestion. If it's something you need to do monthly, do it once and schedule it for next month on your calendar. When you've completed all suggested actions and fully integrated the chosen idea into your thoughts and your life, it's time to move on to the next one, but be sure you continue to practice all new habits. Meanwhile, keep a journal in which you track your progress.

As you begin to implement these ideas one at a time, you may be surprised at how much clutter even small changes can eliminate. Family therapists have long since recognized that minor changes can sometimes trigger huge chain reactions that affect a whole family system, and this principle applies to person-environment systems as well.

Suppose, for example, that mountains of mail have historically occupied your dining room table. Although you occasionally clear it off, much of the time you're unable to use the table for its intended purpose. Then one day you decide to move your recycle bin from the back stairway to a new spot next to the front door. This makes it easier to get rid of junk mail right away, and you establish a new habit of doing so. Now the piles of mail on your table are much smaller, and consequently you get them off the table and into your sorting system much sooner. This enables you to use your table to eat meals with your family, which means that dishes are no longer all over the house, which makes it easier to gather them up and wash them immediately after each meal. A significant amount of mail-clutter and dish-clutter have disappeared from your life, all because you moved a single recycle bin to a different spot.

As each new statement becomes part of your thinking and each new behavior becomes part of your repertoire, you'll see the piles of Things that had been creeping back into your living space grow smaller day by day. Freed from cycles of clutter and de-cluttering, you'll experience a life that runs more smoothly, no longer impeded by time-consuming, frantic searches. You'll feel proud of the way your space looks and enjoy entertaining others in it. Best of all, you'll be able to devote more time and energy to the people and activities you love most. You'll be living clutter-free every day.

One note on the text: While stylistically this book is simpler and more straightforward than my first book, *Making Peace with the Things in Your Life,* I've kept the nonstandard capitalization of the word *Thing* to mean a personal possession, as opposed to *thing,* which I use only as an all-purpose indefinite noun. The original use of *Thing* relates to the pervasive human tendency to personify the objects closest to us. Although such personification is less central to *One Thing at a Time,* for purposes of continuity I've chosen to capitalize *Things* in this book as well.

1. ONE THING AT A TIME.

Do you have one of those brains that goes naturally in twenty-seven directions at once? If so, you may be great at multitasking but susceptible to getting overwhelmed in response to a mess. Instead of focusing on the vase you're about to put back on the shelf, you glance vacantly around at the scummy goldfish bowl, the papers piled on the desk, the kitty litter on the carpet, everywhere and anywhere except at the object in your hands. Because your brain does this, even a small amount of clutter can make you feel as helpless as the princess contemplating the enormous pile of straw that Rumpelstiltskin demanded she spin into gold. The result is paralysis.

This can go on for hours—unless a perceptive person walks over and touches your arm, directs your attention to the vase in your hands, and murmurs a single sentence: *One Thing at a time*. When this happens, your thoughts stop crisscrossing, your body shifts back into action, and progress resumes. The vase goes onto the mantelpiece, your hands reach for the next item, and soon the clutter has disappeared. These five magic little words have the power to release you from even the most profound state of lethargy, overwhelm, or confusion and get you moving again.

Are you too exhausted after a long day's work to deal with the mountain of mail on your counter? Is your basement crammed with items left behind by someone you horribly miss? Do you have absolutely no idea what to do with the stacks of magazines you never have time to read? Does the sight of your dirty dishes make you nauseous? Do you shuffle through papers three or four at a time but never seem to get anywhere with them? The solution to each of these problems is the same: *One Thing at a time*.

As a professional organizer, I've used these words to help clients again and again. Janine was feeling hopeless. She spent much of our first hour talking about how she would never be able to deal with the enormous piles of wrinkled clothes in her bedroom, the sight of which caused her to feel even more depressed. With my encouragement, she finally set to work, but every now and then she would stop and commiserate. Each time she did this, I would repeat the same phrase: "One Thing at a time," and she would get moving again. Eventually her bedroom became clutter-free, which inspired her to go on to other projects.

Hal had problems staying focused. An entrepreneur whose brain was swimming with brilliant new ideas, he attempted to de-clutter his office by rushing around from one pile to another, shuffling through papers and throwing them back down without deciding what to do with any of them. As we continued to work together, Hal began to understand how fruitless this was. As a remedy, he gave me permission to say, "One Thing at a time" each time he started to go off track before completing a project. Eventually he began to say these words to himself. Although Janine and Hal had different problems, the solution for both of them was the same: *One Thing at a time*.

This solution is deceptively simple. The technique of repeating a certain, well-chosen phrase to calm the nerves and focus the mind has worked for millions of people throughout history. Practitioners of most of the world's great religions have used this "mantra" technique for centuries, and people in twelve-step groups find strength in the motto "One day at a time." Whatever clutter-reducing task you're attempting, *One Thing at a time* will help you to stay on track until the job is done.

Write the words on a Post-It or placard and display it wherever you need the reminder. More than any other words in this book, they merit this special status. Make *One Thing at a time* your motto on your journey toward clutter-free living and you'll be amply rewarded.

2. THINGS DON'T MOVE THEMSELVES.

Spontaneous movement is one criterion biologists use to determine what's a form of life and what isn't. Things don't do this. They can move, but not spontaneously: someone or something moves them or they stay where they are. A car, for example, just sits in the driveway until you make it go by moving the key in the ignition and the gas pedal with your foot. Things don't move themselves.

Nevertheless, people often talk about Things as if they're alive and trotting around on little legs. They make statements like "These papers keep piling up," "My clothes always end up on the floor," or "No matter what I do, the clutter always comes back." This kind of thinking compounds the problem, because it implies that you're a powerless victim upon whom your papers and possessions insist on ganging up. It does protect you from having to take action—the mess is all *their* fault and there's nothing you can do about it—but like it or not, everything you own is where it is because you or somebody else put it there. Acknowledging this doesn't mean you have to think of yourself as a bad person; it just means you're free to use your power to put your Things wherever you choose.

Notice what you say about your Things. Do your words imply that you experience them as alive and able to move? If so, try changing the wording from They-statements to I-statements. Do this in writing every day for a week. Change "These papers keep piling up" to "*I* keep piling up these papers," "My clothes always end up on the floor" to "*I* throw my clothes on the floor," and "The clutter keeps coming back" to "*I* keep making more clutter."

As you begin to transform your thoughts into I-statements, feel the power surge that comes with them. Now that you know that *you* are in charge of your Things and not the other way around, there's absolutely no reason you shouldn't rearrange your possessions any way you like. In other words, it's time to get to work!

3. BREATHE, DON'T RUN.

Do piles of random objects scare you? If so, you're no different from a lot of people. The number one cause of big clutter is fear of clutter. Aversion to chaos seems to be wired into most people's brain chemistry along with aversion to snakes. When your brain tries to process the multiple stimuli produced by random objects in space, the system overloads. Add to this a few decades of blaming and shaming for the clutter you keep creating despite your best efforts, and it's not surprising that your palms turn clammy at the sight of a mess.

But being scared doesn't mean you automatically have to run. Running is definitely the wrong thing to do in response to messes. Clutter is like a dragon that gets bigger whenever you run from it. Run from it enough times, and you wind up with big clutter. Turn around and face it, take some long, deep breaths, begin to take action, and watch the clutter disappear.

Try this: Go to the messiest room in your home and stand staring straight into the biggest pile you can find, hands on hips. Don't move, no matter what. How do you feel? Breathe slowly and deeply until you're completely relaxed. What negative or escapist thoughts come up in your head? Every time a new thought comes up, counter it with the word "breathe." *I don't know where to start.* Breathe. *How could I ever let it get like this?* Breathe. *What's the matter with me? I should be able to do this. I'm such a slob.* Breathe. *Maybe I'll just go read.* Breathe. *I can't stand it—in another minute I'm going off to drown my sorrows.* Breathe. Breathe. Breathe. Repeat the word silently in your mind as you breathe slowly in and out and feel the power surge through you. No matter what, don't walk away *or do anything to reduce the clutter* until the negative thoughts have faded into the silence and you feel calm.

As you continue to breathe deeply, you may begin to visualize some kind of constructive action. At first it's just a thought, but as time goes on, it becomes more appealing. Before long you really *want* to put all those old newspapers in the recycle bin. But don't give into the urge right away. Instead, keep breathing slowly in and out. The longer you do this, the harder it becomes *not* to take care of the newspapers.

When you can't stand it anymore, you're ready to proceed.

4. DE-CLUTTER YOUR BODY.

Maybe you don't need this one. Maybe you already get up every morning and shower, wash your hair, brush your teeth, shave or put on make-up, and dress nicely, even though you're planning to spend the day cleaning out your kitchen cupboards. But maybe you don't. Maybe you drag around in a ratty old sweatshirt, avoiding mirrors, and stick a hand out from between the doors so the UPS delivery person won't see you. Not that you're ugly—we both know you could look great if you tried—but you figure appearance doesn't matter when you're planning to spend the day with only rows of canned goods for companions.

If you want to live clutter-free, it *does* matter, because your body is part of the environment you've created. Why go to the trouble of lining up all your books in alphabetical order, polishing the chandelier, and putting fresh flowers on the table if a slovenly, raggedy person is smack in the middle of it all, spoiling the effect? Besides, if you feel good about the way you look, you'll feel more like maintaining good-looking surroundings to match this good-looking person you've become. On an unconscious level, the mind is always trying to resolve dissonance and make things match. Creating order and beauty on one level makes it more likely that you'll create it on another level. It's the old school-uniform concept: when children wear nice, neat uniforms to school, the hope is that they will be more likely to write nice, neat book reports, add up nice, neat columns of figures, and behave in nice, neat ways toward their teachers and friends.

Of course, looking good at home doesn't mean the same thing as looking good in an office. It isn't necessary to put on a three-piece suit or high heels to tackle your worst closet or crawl spaces. But if a professional organizer arrived looking like he or she had just been dragged out of a swamp, how much faith would you have in that person's expertise?

Have some fun creating a spiffy new housework "uniform." If you sew, you're in a position to really experiment; if not, do some creative shopping. Some possibilities: a crisp blue work shirt, a red bandana, and jeans; a colorful coverall or pair of overalls and shirt; an old-fashioned flowered "housedress" or a fifties shirtwaist; a pair of neat blue Chinese pajamas; a painter's smock; a comfy jogging suit; a mumu; a frilly apron; a snazzy halter and shorts. Whatever you wear should be washable and attractive. If it's dirty when you're finished for the day, pop it in the washer so it will be ready for your next job.

Then enjoy a hot soak and get dressed for whatever's next.

5. CARRY A CLIPBOARD.

If you don't have one, go out and buy or borrow one. Then bring it home, clip a yellow legal tablet onto it, go find some clutter, and stand there holding the clipboard, pen in hand. Set the clipboard down for a moment, then pick it up again and feel the difference. Holding a clipboard puts you in the same league with your gym teacher, your camp counselor, or your army sergeant—the person who checks off names and shouts instructions. A clipboard means authority. Face your possessions with a clipboard in your hands, and there's no way they're going to run over you. A clipboard puts you squarely in charge of the Things in your life.

The clipboard will help you feel in control and organized. Carry it when you tour your space, which you should do at least once a month. Yes, I know it's *your* house—you've seen it hundreds of times—but touring your space on a regular basis will help you to view it from a detached perspective and identify problems that need to be addressed. Clipboard in hand, imagine you're a professional organizer looking at a home for the first time. Stand in the doorway of each room and scan systematically around the walls, then the four quadrants of the floor. What's already working? What still needs to be done? What looks terrific? What looks terrible? Make a to-do list on your clipboard of major projects. Include not only de-cluttering and organizing projects but also cleaning, repairing, decorating, and replacing.

You can also use your clipboard to command respect when others in your household are derelict in their duties. Making excuses to a person who stands there jotting things down and looking industrious is a lot harder than making excuses to someone who just stands there with drooping arms. Confronted with a bolt upright clipboard carrier, the offending party is almost guaranteed to blush, stutter, and steal away to put things right. Then you can check the box next to "remind so-and-so" and get on with your day. Be sure to create a convenient home for your clipboard and put it there whenever you finish using it.

6. POST CHECKLISTS OF
ROUTINE TASKS.

There are two kinds of clutter-reducing household tasks: routine and one-time. Routine tasks are performed at regular intervals: making beds, doing dishes, dusting, sweeping, cleaning out the hamster cage. An awful lot of clutter happens purely because routine tasks either don't get done at all or are abandoned unfinished, leaving a lot of Things lying around. Unwashed dishes make dish clutter; unfinished laundry makes clothes clutter; unfiled papers make paper clutter; uncleaned hamster cages make hamster-cage clutter. When people fail to accomplish routine tasks, they might have only a vague sense of what jobs need to be done. To keep from creating clutter on a daily basis, it's essential to get your routine tasks clearly in your head.

Checklists are an invaluable tool for clarifying routine tasks. Make at least four of them: daily, weekly, monthly, and annual. I recommend creating each list on a separate piece of paper and posting them all in a central place. Keep the lists simple and make sure they're easy to read. For example:

DAILY

☐ Make beds

☐ Hang up clothes

☐ Breakfast dishes

☐ Dinner dishes

☐ Sort papers

- ☐ Dust, sweep, and vacuum living room
- ☐ Clean bathroom
- ☐ Clean out hamster cage
- ☐ Take out trash

WEEKLY

- ☐ Clean out refrigerator
- ☐ Grocery shop
- ☐ Put groceries away
- ☐ Mop kitchen floor
- ☐ Dust, sweep, and vacuum whole house
- ☐ Wash clothes
- ☐ Sort and fold clothes
- ☐ Sweep back porch
- ☐ Hose off patio
- ☐ File papers
- ☐ Sort recyclables

MONTHLY

- ☐ Clean oven
- ☐ Pay bills
- ☐ Take unwanted items to charities
- ☐ Clean mirrors

☐ Wash windows

☐ Turn mattresses

☐ Clean out kitchen cupboards

☐ Clean out bedroom drawers and closets

☐ Purge files

☐ Clean out garage

☐ Clean out basement

The above lists are just examples; your own lists may have different routine tasks on them and a different timetable, depending on your circumstances. Note that posting a checklist doesn't mean you'll always choose to do every task on it when the time comes. You may decide, for example, that the refrigerator doesn't need cleaning this week and you'd rather spend your time catching up on letter-writing or something else you've been meaning to do. But the checklists form a general outline of your goals and intentions.

If other people in your household share tasks, write the name of the person responsible next to each task and ask others to help make the lists. In that case, you might also post a list of the proper steps for each job near where it's done, such as, a list of steps in the bathroom for cleaning the bathroom; a list of steps in the kitchen for doing dishes or cleaning the stove; a list of steps in the broom closet for cleaning the floors. Writing out these steps enables the reader to visualize the "actions" that the task involves, making the job less overwhelming and easier to perform. When I was in college, I lived in a co-op where we did this, and it worked wonderfully. Doing a job that had already been broken down into steps was virtually painless. Rotating jobs and having several people share a job also helps to reduce monotony.

7. ROLL BACK YOUR SLEEP SCHEDULE BY HALF AN HOUR.

Many self-help book authors advise you to get up half an hour earlier to make time for whatever it is they're helping you to do. Although this may be a good idea, it probably won't happen if you don't also go to bed half an hour earlier, nor should it. Early to rise without early to bed is a great way to end up sleep-deprived, which puts your health and safety at risk, and it certainly won't make you more organized, productive, or clear-headed. Rolling your whole sleep schedule back half an hour, however, will not hurt you and may even put you on the path to better health. It's also likely to reduce the amount of clutter in your home—and possibly at work as well.

Each of us has his or her own, individualized circadian rhythms, and early to bed, early to rise might not be feasible for everyone. But for those who can manage it, an extra thirty minutes in the morning, during which beds can be made, clothes hung up, dishes washed, and living space tidied, can make the difference between chaos and order. When people who work outside the home race off without accomplishing these tasks, clutter accumulates. On the other hand, those who leave a clean, orderly living space behind them can let go of concerns about housework and even feel more motivated to create order in their workplace.

If getting to bed earlier so as to get up earlier is difficult for you, try to roll as much of your evening back as you can. What activities earlier in the evening wouldn't you miss? Is there some way you could combine several? Perhaps you could let go of a TV series you habitually watch (or sort through papers while you watch it), buy a newspaper to read on the train instead of at home, or settle for simpler meals that take less time to prepare.

Establishing an earlier bedtime may also involve retraining those near and dear to you. Let others know that you'll no longer be taking calls after a particular time, and if the phone rings after hours, let it (see #26). Put children to bed half an hour sooner—they'll get used to it quickly, and they'll be better organized for school or play in the morning. Ask for your significant other's help in settling down a little earlier.

Always remember that nobody but *you* controls how you spend your time—so it's well worth considering the full field of options and the big effects a little change can make.

8. STOP PERFECTING, START BETTERING.

Years ago I was a violin student. When practicing I would often become stuck on a difficult line, unable to go forward and learn the rest of the piece until I'd perfected the passage, which was usually impossible. By the day of my lesson I might almost be able to play the challenging line, but I'd have to sight-read the rest of the piece. The resulting chaos gave my teacher, a tyrannical little professor of music, the impression that I never practiced at all. Then one morning, desperate to avoid another of the professor's tirades, I broke the pattern. I was in my practice room sawing away at the trouble spot, becoming more and more frustrated, when suddenly a voice in my head offered four little words as a gift: *Stop perfecting, start bettering*. From then on, each time I repeated a difficult passage, I'd try to play it better than the time before. If I missed fewer notes or played with a purer tone or added some new dynamics, I went on to the next line. Needless to say, my lessons became less disastrous.

Ironically enough, perfectionism often seems to carry us further away from perfection than simply aiming for progress. Such is the case when your goal is to live *more* clutter-free. Devoting your every waking hour to keeping every object in its place at all times is dangerous. Eventually you're going to burn out, and possibly even go to the opposite extreme and refuse to put away anything at all for the next six months. Such is the path to self-perpetuating cycles of "clutter bulimia."

When you try to maintain a perfectionistic approach, you also risk getting stuck, as I did with the violin, focusing on one part of a task and ignoring the rest. If you're a perfectionist, and you have only an hour to spend on a cluttered room, instead of significantly bettering your surroundings by hauling away a few large items and throwing loose papers into a box, you open up an envelope filled with receipts and spend the time arranging them in alphabetical order.

Next time you find yourself falling into a perfectionistic mode, notice how your body feels. Do your muscles feel tense? Is there a knot in your stomach? Now take a deep breath and shift gears. Forget about the Martha Stewart room that you'll never be able to quite create and spend five minutes bettering the real room around you. Doesn't that feel healthier? Perfectionism is hazardous to your well-being. Bettering, on the other hand, will always leave you feeling energized and ready to do more. Only bettering, not perfectionism, will enable you to permanently live more clutter-free.

9. MAKE YOUR BED EVERY DAY.

Once, while studying meditation at a Zen Buddhist temple, I was instructed to choose a simple daily task and try to perform it as mindfully as possible. I chose making my bed as the task, and it has never been the same experience since. Whatever your religious or spiritual practice, try to make daily bed-making a part of it. Think of your bed as a holy place, where you receive the gift of sleep as well as messages in the form of dreams. Your bed might be floating on a sea of clutter, but it can become a raft of serenity.

There are all kinds of beds: single beds, double beds, king beds, queen beds, water beds, camp beds, hospital beds, hide-a-beds, four-poster beds, bunk beds, water beds, canopy beds, futons, cots, sleeping bags, and straw ticks. It doesn't matter what kind of bed you have so long as it's firm enough to keep your back healthy. What matters is what you put on the bed and how.

Let's suppose that your bed is standing there with only a bare mattress. Start with a clean mattress pad to protect yourself from buttons and bumps. Smooth it out and pull it tight. Then add a fitted sheet and do the same thing, or make "hospital corners" with a flat bottom sheet. The top sheet goes on face down so the pattern will show when you fold the top over the blankets as well as when you're between the sheets. Sheets that have been washed and dried in the sunlight may transport you back to an idyllic era reminiscent of porch swings and apple blossoms. Add blankets one by one, as many as you need for the season. Then a quilt, if you have one, preferably handmade. Each time you add another cover, smooth it wrinkle-free. Fold the top sheet down about eight inches and tuck everything in all the way around. Add pillows in fresh pillowcases—embroidered ones are ideal—and a bedspread if you like. Neatly fold an extra blanket, comforter, or afghan and lay it on the foot of the bed. Garnish the bed with small pillows or stuffed animals and stand back to survey your handiwork.

Change your sheets once a week. When you do so, your reward is sleeping on clean sheets that night. The real challenge, however, is to make your bed mindfully every day. Try to focus totally on the process, no matter how many times you've done it before. If you do, you'll enjoy it, and if you enjoy it you'll do it every day, and if you do it every day, you'll render as many square feet as the bed occupies permanently clutter-free.

The secret of daily bed-making, to quote Betty MacDonald's Mrs. Piggle-Wiggle, "is to throw the covers way back." Carelessly dragging all the covers up at once leaves wrinkles all through them. Mindful bed-making means that you smooth out the bottom sheet first, then smooth out the wrinkles of each cover one by one as you pull it up. Smoothing covers gives you a lovely feeling once you're tuned into it. Breathe in a rush of cool air and let your fingertips soak in the smoothness all along the sheet.

An unmade bed makes a convenient hiding place for dirty tissues and rumpled clothes, but a freshly made bed exerts a positive influence on the whole room. Clothes hanging over chairs or used cocoa cups on the nightstand now seem as out of place as someone wearing dirty overalls to a worship service. You simply *must* do something about them.

The beauty of de-cluttering your bed is that you can do it in relatively little time. It takes just a few minutes to make a large area of your floor space into a pocket of order, an oasis of comfort and a shining example of what a little mindful focus can achieve.

10. OPEN THE WINDOWS.

You know the feeling—the fresh, clean, energized one that only oxygen can give. So open your windows and bring it in. If it's January in Maine or July in Florida, you might be able to stand opening the windows for just a few seconds, but that's OK—do it anyway. Imagine you're in a chalet high in the Swiss Alps shaking out downfilled comforters. Feel the fresh air rush in and chase the must and mold out the open windows.

Human beings breathe in oxygen and breathe out carbon dioxide. When a house stays sealed up for too long, whether it's really the case or not, you *feel* oxygen deprived, your energy flags, and clutter piles up. Plants live on carbon dioxide and excrete oxygen, making the air particularly fresh in their vicinity. If you want to get the benefits of the oxygen produced by the plants and trees in your yard, allow the air to flow unimpeded into your house.

Take it from one with German hausfraus on her family tree: combining fresh air with bed-making can be wonderful. So can "airing out" the bedding. Although certain laundry detergents and additives purport to re-create the smell of sunlight-dried sheets and blankets, nothing has quite the same effect as the real thing.

As you invite more air into your life, don't be surprised if more order sweeps in along with it. Although only you can pick up objects and put them where you choose, getting musty old air flowing out of your space may motivate you to get musty old objects out too. Less stuff means more room for life-giving air, and a few deep breaths will energize you to keep wonderful new spaces clutter-free.

11. MAKE A LIST OF
MINITASKS.

Unaccomplished minitasks are a common source of clutter. A three-minute call will get your washer fixed, but you keep putting it off while the dirty clothes spill out of hampers. It would take five minutes to sew the button on the shirt that has been hanging over the footboard of your bed for six months. The books you threw on the office floor when you wrote your last article three weeks ago just need to go back on the shelves—not a big deal—but there they sit.

If you're a certain kind of person, you may neglect small chores simply because they *are* small. Piddly little tasks don't interest you— if you're going to do a job, it needs to be a *real* job, a job you can sink your teeth into, a job that will give you a sense of accomplishment to have finished.

If that's where you're coming from, the secret is to pool your minitasks by making a long list of them and then throw yourself into the big job of doing them all, one after another. You may even want to declare a whole day "minitask day." To qualify, the job should take ten minutes or less. Many will take only a minute or two. Some possible candidates:

- Sort mail

- Make a phone call

- Fill out an insurance form

- Write a check

- Address an envelope

- Send an e-mail

- Check a Web site

- Skim an article

- Carry something upstairs, downstairs, or out to the car

- Wipe up something that's spilled

- Fold a blanket or towel

- Fold up a newspaper

- Hang up a piece of clothing

- Sew on a button

- Gather up cups and glassware

- Put trash in the trash can

- Take out the trash

- Brush the dog

- Wash out the dog's dish

- Change the kitty litter

- Rinse out the diaper pail

- Rinse out a pair of stockings

- Knock down cobwebs

- Put a book back on the shelf

- Shine shoes

- Clean a mirror

- Wash the mats in your car

- Clean your glasses

- Wipe off fingerprints

Once you've worked your way through a list of minitasks, reward yourself just as you would if you'd finished one big job. Walk around and look at all the small changes you've made. Notice how much freer you feel now that you're no longer trying to keep track of so many unfinished little projects. Small as each of them is, collectively they can take their toll on you. Chances are, unfinished minitasks have been sapping your precious energy for a long time, but no more.

Resolve to keep an ongoing list of minitasks someplace—in your planner, on your refrigerator, on your bulletin board—and clear it every week on "minitask day." If you do this regularly you'll soon become not only more clutter-free, but more stress-free as well.

12. STEM THE PAPER INFLOW.

The more paper you can keep from entering your home, the less paper clutter you'll be likely to have. Stemming the inflow significantly involves a number of small tasks that you can do one or two at a time:

- Write the Mail Preference Service (P.O. Box 9008, Farmingdale, NY 11735-9008) and ask that your name not be sold to any mailing list companies.

- Consider the newspapers and magazines you subscribe to. How often do you read them? Cancel or let lapse any subscriptions for periodicals you haven't read in over six months. When newspapers arrive, immediately dump all the loose advertising inserts into the recycle bin.

- Invest a little time and money that may save you trouble in the long run. Buy 100 stamped postcards. For the next month, each time you receive a piece of junk mail from an outfit that has frequently contacted you, send its employees a postcard pointing out that they're wasting money and asking to be removed from their mailing list. If the junk mail contains a 1-800 number or an e-mail address, use these means to contact them as well. Some businesses will ignore your request and continue to send you unwanted mail, but others will get the message. Dump all junk mail into the recycle bin as soon as it comes in the door.

- Register at www.emailpreferenceservice.com to stem the e-mail tide. In addition, be selective about what e-mail you choose to print out. A few important messages may be worth the space in your paper files, but many are not. Leave these messages filed on your hard disk and save a few trees (and your precious space).

- Stop bringing home excess freebee papers. Before you leave a conference, purge the papers you've collected and take home only those that are genuinely helpful. Leave your church program at church, your concert program at the concert, your museum map at the museum, and respond with a polite "No, thank you" to people handing out leaflets on the street.

13. ALPHABETIZE.

I know it's obvious, but so often we don't think to do it when we could. Alphabetizing is appropriate any time you're organizing a lot of little Things with words on them. Papers, of course. But also books, magazines, spices, paint jars, and all sorts of collectibles. Objects that don't already have words on them can, of course, be alphabetized if you put labels on them yourself.

In organizing papers, many people automatically think categories. This is fine as long as there aren't too many categories. But you can save a lot of time if, within each category, you alphabetize the folders. In the hanging file folder labeled "Insurance," for example, individual file folders are arranged as "Auto Insurance," "Boat Insurance," "Homeowners' Insurance," or "Life Insurance" instead of in random order. Some people who have trouble thinking in categories do best if they forego categories altogether and alphabetize everything from A to Z.

Alphabetizing your books takes time, but it's worth the effort. In libraries, novels are organized alphabetically by the author's last name. Nonfiction books are organized in categories that are each given a number, but within each category they, like fiction books, are alphabetized by author. While you may not need to use the Dewey decimal system to find books in your own home, following the same general principles can save you hours of looking for lost volumes and reduce the amount of book clutter in your space.

Physically, the task of alphabetizing a lot of books can be daunting, as each time you put in a new book by an author whose last name comes early in the alphabet, you end up shoving some books along a single shelf and moving others down to the next shelf. To make the job easier, divide 26 by the number of shelves you expect to use for a group of books. Suppose you have eight shelves, for example. Twenty-six divided by eight is 3.25, which can be rounded off to three. Thus, approximately three letters' worth of books will go on each shelf. Put a sticky note on each shelf with the appropriate letters for that shelf: *ABC, DEF, GHI, JKL, MNO, PQR, STU, VWXYZ*. Then remove all the books from each shelf that don't belong there and put the ones that remain in alphabetical order. Each time you pick up a volume from the piles on the floor, put it on the appropriate shelf. When a shelf fills up, you'll have to readjust, but this will require a lot less effort than alphabetizing without previously breaking things down.

If you're dyslexic, alphabetizing may not be the best organizing strategy for you (instead, sort by colors, size, picture labels or other nongraphic means). Otherwise, alphabetizing not only makes Things easier to find but also makes them easier to put away. The easier it is to put Things away, the more likely that you—and others—will do so, and the more Things you put away, the fewer items remain in piles, cluttering up your life.

14. SPEED UP YOUR HEART.

Some clutter piles happen because people feel too lethargic to habitually put Things back after they use them. Other piles happen because people can't seem to stay focused. A terrific solution to both problems is aerobic exercise. Something about getting your heart pumping hard and taking in lots of air seems to do wonders for both your mood and your ability to attend to tasks. I once heard a well-known psychiatrist say that when you exercise aerobically, it's as though you've taken a little Prozac and a little Ritalin. The best part is, if you choose a form of aerobic exercise that's appropriate for your age and physique and break into it gradually, it will help your body as well as your mind and spirit (and your space).

For exercise to have the maximum effect on your daily life—and thus help to eliminate clutter—get your heart pumping first thing in the morning. It doesn't have to be of long duration to have a significant impact. Fifteen or twenty minutes of jogging, brisk walking, or stair climbing is all you need to wake up your brain—and it is healthier than caffeine. (If you want to lose weight, you'll have to do more, alas.) Take a quick, refreshing shower afterwards and you'll be ready to go.

Mental fatigue and physical fatigue are interrelated. If you run out of steam after emptying out your closet or feel that you simply can't go on filing papers, take an exercise break. Jog around the block or climb the stairs a few times, then get back to work with a fresh flow of energy and a clear head. If the exercise break doesn't seem to help, you may be genuinely tired and need a short nap, or hungry and need a snack before you can revive.

Sometimes housework itself can be exercise, especially if you push yourself a little. Shove the vacuum cleaner around, bob and bend as you scrub out the shower, jog in and out of the garage as you empty it. Then have a nice, big glass of water and reward yourself by shifting to a more peaceful task.

15. DESIGNATE AN ERRAND DAY.

I don't have time to get organized," you complain.

Since you, like everyone, have only twenty-four hours in each day, you need to find a way to free up some time from another activity. One thing to consider is the frequency with which you do errands. Are you going to your bank, post office, pharmacy, dry cleaners, hardware store, supermarket, and copy center almost every day? If so, you may be wasting a lot of time coming and going that you could use to keep your space free of clutter. To reclaim that time, designate one day in your week "Errand Day" or, if you have to do a lot of errands for others as well as yourself, perhaps two days.

Reclaiming this time means you'll sometimes have to delay gratification—that is—wait. If you're used to impulsively going out whenever an errand thought crosses your mind, this will not be easy. Post an errand list on your refrigerator. Every time you think of an errand you need to do, instead of racing off to do it right away, write it down on the list. Then tell yourself that it will be just X number of days before the errand will be done. Of course, some errands are emergencies and must be done immediately, but most can wait.

You may also have to reprogram others' expectations. If you've become the errand girl or boy for your family, inform them that you're trying to consolidate your errands in order to make more time for getting organized, and ask for their help. Tell them when your errand day will be, show them your errand list, and invite them to add errands that you're willing to do for them. Then, instead of jumping whenever family members snap their fingers, issue reminders about your new system. And try not to do any errand that someone else can do.

It could be useful to determine exactly how much time you save by having an errand day. To accomplish this, do errands spontaneously for a couple of weeks and keep track of all the time you spend, from the moment you leave your house to the moment you return home again. Then choose your errand day, post your list, inform your family, and keep track of your time for two more weeks. Compare the amount of errand time for each two weeks. The difference is your time dividend.

When your errand day arrives, be systematic in your approach. Take your posted list and number the errands in the order you want to do them, in accordance with geography so that you won't need to backtrack. If you like, make a rough map and plot in the location of each errand. Set out early to avoid traffic. Above all, relish the feeling of each necessary errand efficiently accomplished, with newfound time to spare.

16. THAT WAS THEN, THIS IS NOW.

For over twenty years, I hung onto my old college sociology textbook. Heaven knows why. The book had served me well in my introductory course, after which I never looked at it again. I did not become a sociologist, and if I had, I would have wanted something more advanced and up-to-date. Yet year after year, there it was on the shelf, taking up space between my old psych book and my old poli sci book, transported through three or four moves before it finally occurred to me to put it, along with the other outdated textbooks, in a box for the public library book sale. Back in college I had needed the book, but as an ex–sociology student, I didn't. What was adaptive in those circumstances was maladaptive in my current circumstances. That was then, this is now.

Perhaps the biggest obstacle to living clutter-free is our failure to recognize how circumstances have changed. As a professional organizer, I've worked with people who moved out of a big house into a small apartment and tried to take everything with them. I've seen affluent individuals who grew up in poverty continue to act impoverished by hoarding items of little or no value as if their survival depended upon them. I've helped clients who hung onto possessions of a loved one who has died or otherwise left, unable to face their loss and let go. All of these people needed help catching up with the realities of the present. So do most of us at some time or another. Stuff piles up, like my old textbooks, because we forget to ask ourselves if we still need Things now that we needed before.

Hanging onto old Things is only one means, however, by which enslavement to the past may create piles. A far more pernicious cause of major clutter is the failure to realize that you've grown up. As an infant, you started out unable to affect your immediate surroundings much at all. You could do nothing but lie in your crib wailing and kicking your legs in the air. Then you sat up, gurgled, cooed, crawled, knocked over milk cups, and threw your Cheerios on the floor. Whenever you engaged in such self-assertive behaviors, giant arms came down and interfered. You still had almost no power. Everything you owned was given to you by someone else who could also take it away. Sometimes your caregivers met your needs; at other times they did not, leaving a void that Things—especially warm, fuzzy Things—helped to fill. Perhaps caregivers even caused you pain, so you clung to Things for comfort, which sort of worked—*then*.

Now you're an adult who can pick up objects in a coordinated fashion and move them wherever you like, not a helpless infant at the mercy of the Things in your life and the grown-ups who control them. Now you can consider the complexities of your present situation and decide which objects are useful and important to you and how best to arrange and maintain them. Now you can cultivate healthy relationships with others rather than hanging onto objects as people-substitutes. What you did in the past worked then; if you try to do it now in different circumstances it may not work at all. Now, in the present, you need a new set of coping strategies—and a new assortment of Things. That was then, this is now.

17. GET A ROLODEX.

The Rolodex is a marvelous invention. It can eliminate those little scraps of paper all over the house with phone numbers and addresses written on them, as well as the multitudinous business cards packed into your wallet. Some Rolodexes are round, while others are flat trays. The round ones typically hold more cards but are more awkward to use than the flat trays. Many hold three-by-five-inch cards, but some hold smaller ones. The larger cards are definitely worth the extra money, as you can staple a business card onto a three-by-five-inch card and still have room to jot down other information. Cards are available in all sorts of snazzy colors, and you can get special cards with slots for business cards. The standard, brand-name Rolodex includes alphabet tabs, but special index tabs are also available for household categories such as Baby-sitters, Emergency, and Medical. My Rolodex of choice is a flat tray with three-by-five-inch cards. I've been using it for years and would be lost without it.

The advantage of the Rolodex over the old-fashioned address book—or address pages in your planner—is flexibility: you can put a lot more information on cards, staple in business cards, rearrange cards to keep them alphabetical, and pull out cards to take with you when you go on a trip. The ideal entry includes e-mail, Web site, and fax number as well as name, address, and phone number(s). In most cases you'll file your cards by the person's or organization's name, but you may also want to make some group cards for individuals of a particular category. In my own Rolodex, I have group cards for carpenters, electricians, house cleaners, handymen, plumbers, therapists, and psychiatrists—all professionals to whom I may refer clients.

If you're an e-person rather than a paper person, you may prefer to use an electronic contact management system. Computer programs such as Outlook allow you to type in contact information, as do Personal Digital Assistants (PDAs) such as Palm Pilots, and many cell phones. Keeping phone numbers and addresses only in a desktop PC is not convenient unless you spend virtually all of your time where your computer is and keep it constantly booted up. If you have the right type of pocket device, however, you can feed computer information into it. PDAs are handy and can do all sorts of amazing things but, like computers, they carry the risk of crashing and wiping out all your information. If you use any kind of "e-Rolodex," it's important to back up whatever's on it with a hard copy.

Whatever form of Rolodex you use, the trick is to *use* it. Any time you look up a number in the phone book, ask yourself if you're likely to call that number again. A little voice may be saying "Later," but ignore it and copy the name, address, and number into the Rolodex *now*. Or make a special basket, cubby, or accordion folder in your paper management system and label it "Rolodex." Whenever someone gives you a business card or e-mails you contact information, pop it into this pre-Rolodex file. Then, once a month or so, clear it out and transfer everything into the Rolodex. And from time to time, purge your entries: ask yourself how likely it is that you'll need to contact someone again, and if it's unlikely, scrap the entry.

18. KEEP THE CLOTHES MOVING ON.

If they're on the floor, put them in the hamper. If they're in the hamper, put them in the laundry baskets. If they're in the laundry baskets, put them in the washer. If they're in the washer, put them in the dryer. If they're in the dryer, hang them on the line or fold them and put them back in the laundry baskets. If they're on the line or in the laundry baskets, put them in the closets and the drawers. Clothes that get stuck somewhere in the laundry cycle create big mounds of clothes clutter, all of which can be easily removed. Just keep the clothes moving until they're all back in closets and drawers and watch the piles disappear.

You also need to ask where the clothes get stuck and why. If you tend to throw clothes on the floor, make sure you have an attractive hamper that's big enough and easy to use. If you're slow to get clothes into the washer, is it because you're forever running out of detergent, never have quarters handy, or are afraid of dying your white underclothes purple or shrinking your favorite sweater? Stock up on laundry supplies and address your fears by reading labels on clothes and detergents.

Do you prematurely declare the job done just because the clothes are dry? In that case, how do you feel about folding clothes? Does the task bore you unbearably or make you feel like a slave? If so, reframe it as a form of meditation. Folding and hanging up laundry, like bed-making (see #9), are great Zen chores. If you don't do this as soon as you take the clothes out, no wonder you hate it. Clothes fresh out of the dryer can give you a lift; those that have been balled up in a basket for three days, on the other hand, can make you feel burdened and discouraged (and you'll have wrinkled clothes).

Laundry is one of those tasks that fits easily between other tasks.

The trick is to get into the habit of taking laundry breaks throughout your day and/or evening. You come back from meeting with a client, then move the clothes on. You finish a meal, then move the clothes on. You spend two hours on paperwork, then move the clothes on. You watch a TV program until the commercials start, then move the clothes on.

If you've worked in a clothing store or spent a significant amount of time in a laundromat, you know that there's an art to folding clothes. Shake the wrinkles out of shirts and hang them up, make "sock balls," bring the corners of sheets together, and fold in the arms of T-shirts and tuck up the bottoms the way they were when you bought them. The more you do this, the more skilled you become. Who knows, you might even want to try your hand at ironing. As you become more skilled at clean-clothes management yourself, you might enlist the help of your kids. Even a young child can enjoy rolling up socks, and handling laundry trains the brain to sort and categorize. If you find sorting laundry difficult, this may be because your own brain has a sorting and categorizing glitch, brilliant though it may be in other areas. It never feels good to do something difficult, and if that's the case for you, it may be worth asking or paying someone else to do your laundry. Dropping it off at the laundromat may well be worth the extra expense.

The laundry cycle is not the only place where clothes can get stuck: excess clothes may also get stuck on their way out of the house. Is your closet packed with clothes you haven't worn since junior high? Are your drawers filled with odd socks? Do you fill bags with garments to give away and then leave the bags for six months on your bedroom floor or next to the front door or in the garage or in your car? Keep those clothes moving on!

19. THROW AWAY COUPONS.

In my ideal world, there would be no such thing as coupons. Nor would there be little plastic cards with points for special club members or rebate slips that have to be mailed back in. Not only are most of these mechanisms tricks to keep consumers believing businesses are being generous when they're not—most of these "money-saving" features simply result in higher prices to begin with—but they're also difficult for many people to keep track of. Anyone with a busy schedule or a nonlinear thinking style, not to mention attention deficit disorder, dyslexia, head trauma, stroke, dementia, or Alzheimer's is likely to become overwhelmed by these complex shopping schemes and lose out. So are any of the rest of us who don't wish to make shopping a full-time profession.

Handling coupons is detail work. Few of us possess the brain style and free time needed to scan through the dozens of coupons that arrive via mail, e-mail, newspapers, and magazines, pick out those we may use, keep track of expiration dates, and make sure we have the right coupons with us to buy the right products at the right time.

Yet many try, and the result is countertops buried under unused, outdated coupons and a feeling of having failed. What lurks behind these piles is the fear that you might possibly pay a few cents—or even a few dollars—more than you need to for something. But what cost do you pay in effort, time, and clutter? Do yourself a favor: face your fears and let the coupons go.

If, despite what I've said, you're determined to keep coupons anyway, at least try to be selective. Get rid of all grocery coupons for foods that lack nutritional value or are filled with bad fats and harmful chemicals, which at most standard supermarkets include a high percentage of the items on the shelves. Then get rid of coupons for dry clearners on the other side of town, oil-change places with bad reputations, and spas you know you'll never actually visit. Keep only coupons for products you frequently use and put them in your wallet, where you're most likely to find them when you're at the checkout counter. Do this for a couple of months, then ask yourself how many coupons you've actually used. If it's a reasonable number, fine. If not, next time you're tempted to set yourself up for failure by hanging on to a bunch of coupons, be nice to yourself and throw them away.

20. MAKE A HOME FOR INSTRUCTIONS AND WARRANTEES.

It can be a box. It can be a drawer. It can be a pocket folder. It can be a file. It doesn't matter what the home is for your instructions and warrantees as long as there is only one and it's easy to reach. Making a single home for the paperwork that goes with the machines in your life will save you hours of turning the house upside down looking for it. More importantly, you won't be so likely to deposit a newly broken appliance on the basement shelf next to thirty others—all waiting until you have time to look for *their* manuals—and go buy another one. Lost documentation is a common cause of broken-machine overpopulation.

I recommend keeping your machine documents in whatever room most of your appliances are in—the kitchen, the TV room, or the home office. Organizing the instructions and warrantees within the container is optional. If you want to go further, you can have separate containers for instructions and warrantees, or even categorize and/or alphabetize the contents. Once a year you should purge out all the paperwork for machines you no longer have.

If you should give an appliance away or sell it, be sure to hand over the instructions—and the warranty, if it's still valid—along with the machine.

21. LOOK WHAT I JUST DID.

Did you just finish making your bed, rearranging your books, or cleaning out a closet? If so, don't rush into the next project. Instead, stand back and look at what you just did. Doing so is vitally important if you're going to both maintain the pocket of order you've created and move on to create more pockets.

Psychological research has shown that positive reinforcement is far more effective than negative reinforcement in bringing about permanent changes in behavior. If you're working by yourself, *you* are the only one who can give yourself pats on the back for what you accomplish. If someone is helping you with de-cluttering, part of that person's job should be to rave about even your smallest successes. The more you allow yourself to appreciate what you've done, and the more encouragement you receive from others, the more motivated you'll feel to do more.

Not that you have to drown yourself in praise—you just have to *take in* what you've done instead of letting it slip by you. Suppose you just cleared the last two weeks' worth of mail from your dining room table and sorted them into "to file" and "action" baskets. Now the table is clean. Wipe off crumbs and dust with a damp sponge and polish the surface until it shines. Run your fingers along the smooth surface and savor the feeling. Stand back and admire its glow.

Now use the area for its intended purpose. Lay out some placemats, arrange a centerpiece—if only a single candle or a small vase. Then sit down and have a snack or at least a glass of water at the table. Promise yourself that you'll continue to use the table in this way at every meal. Consider rewarding yourself by buying some new placemats or flowers.

If and when a member of your cheering section comes home or

stops by to visit, tell the person proudly what you did and enjoy any oohs and ahs that result. If anyone says something critical, counter it immediately with assertive words such as "You're entitled to your opinion, but I'm still proud of what I did." (This might be someone to drop from your support system!)

When you're by yourself again, look in the mirror, imagine a crowd applauding you for taking care of yourself, and take a bow.

22. DECLARE A FIX-IT DAY.

Broken Things invite procrastination. Broken Things cannot be used. Broken Things are clutter until they're fixed. Fixing takes time and so does calling repair people or going to the repair shop. Consequently, broken Things have a way of piling up. Emotional issues may also be involved, because people are not always nice to each other when Things get broken.

Perhaps you remember breaking something accidentally during your childhood and some nasty grown-up snarling, "If you'd just taken proper care, this wouldn't have happened. Why are you always so careless?" The angry words left you feeling that any time something breaks it must be your fault, although frequently it's not. It helps to remind yourself that even when you *are* at fault, you're human and allowed to make mistakes. People who blame others unfairly when Things break are too weak themselves to face the harsh reality of an unpredictable universe in which accidents can happen, no matter how careful we try to be.

Once every six months or so, declare a Fix-It Day. The purpose of this day is to deal with absolutely anything in your home that doesn't work. Schedule it on your calendar. The goal is that by the end of the day all these broken Things will be either gone, fixed, or on their way to being repaired. Broken Things include not only broken appliances, but china angels with one wing off, light bulbs that need changing, split window screens, shirts with torn seams, cracked mirrors, Teddy bears with missing eyes, and shoes with broken heels.

This goal may seem like a tall order, but it's manageable if you break it down. Start your Fix-It Day by walking from room to room—with your clipboard of course—looking for broken Things, gathering up as many of them as you can, and making notes on the rest. Then categorize all of the broken Things into the following:

- Items beyond repair, to either trash or recycle
- Items you can fix yourself
- Items you can take to a repair person
- Items for which a repair person must come to you

Make a list of the broken items that belong in each category and estimate the amount of time you need for each project, whether it involves fixing, calling, or taking an object somewhere. What supplies will you need? Start a shopping list for the hardware store, appliance store, or fabric shop. Also, estimate the cost of having professionals repair items you can't fix yourself. On the basis of your estimates, decide which items you can attend to today and which you must deal with later. If you can't deal with an item today, choose a date when you can, and write this on your calendar, planner, or PDA. Commit to fixing it then.

Then you're ready to get to work. Start by taking away items to be trashed or recycled, making the rounds of repair people, and buying whatever supplies you need to do repairs yourself. Then come home and make calls to repair people who'll come to your home. Finally, get busy fixing Things yourself.

If you live with others, try to involve them in your Fix-It Day, keeping in mind that it is *your* Fix-It Day and they might not be as enthusiastic about it as you are. If someone in your household has been promising to fix the stereo for a long time without doing it, give the person plenty of advance notice about when your Fix-It Day will be, with a warning that if he or she has not fixed it by then, you—or they—will pay someone else to do it. Others might jump on board and you can divvy up the labor; if not, you can deal with broken items yourself and not have to share the power surge you'll experience in discovering that no matter how hopelessly broken something is, you can respond to the problem effectively—and clear your space.

23. WRITE IT DOWN.

Believe it or not, the art of writing can actually keep a lot of would-be clutter from happening. Not just any writing, though. In this case, writing things down *instead of doing something else.*

Fear of forgetting is a common cause of clutter. For most of us, writing serves as a reliable memory aid. Instead of trying to hold all the items in your memory that you'll need to buy at the grocery store, you make a list. If you didn't do this, you'd have to repeat "bananas, green beans, mozzarella, paper towels" all the way to the store and would not be able to think about much else. Having written these items down, you can relax and listen to the news or plan your next vacation on the way. You trust the writing to take care of you. Even if you don't look at your list when you get to the store, you'll probably remember the items better than you otherwise would have because the act of writing has a way of fixing things in your memory.

One situation in which writing may help to intercept needless clutter is when you have a task to do, especially an errand. Instead of writing down the task someplace where you're sure to see it, you may habitually leave an object out to remind yourself of the job: You need to get your prescription refilled, so you leave the medicine bottle out on the counter. You need to take your dog for a walk, so you leave the leash hanging over the doorknob. You need to pay your bills, so you leave them piled on your desk. If you need to do just a few tasks, this isn't a bad way to cope. But if you have a lot on your plate and are also leaving Things out for other reasons, it can make for a mess. Buried under a pile of household items, the "reminder" item no longer serves its purpose.

You can continue in the same self-defeating pattern if you like, or you can do something new: *write*. Next time you're tempted to leave something out as a reminder, try writing the errand down instead. Write it somewhere highly visible—in your planner or PDA if you frequently look at it; at the top of a list on your refrigerator; in big block letters on a piece of paper taped to the door—whatever works. Then put the object itself back in its proper home. You'll feel anxious, of course, but do it anyway. Trust. The written word has been helping people remember things for a long time.

A second situation in which writing something down may avert clutter is when items are hidden away in closed containers. This is especially true in the case of files. You're afraid that you won't be able to remember what papers are in which filing cabinets, so you try to aid your memory by leaving papers out all over your desk instead of filing them away. The result is a mountain of random sheets, none of which you can easily find. A more effective strategy for remembering is to type or write an index of the contents of each file drawer and post it on the outside. That's what those little rectangles above the handles are for.

A third situation in which writing things down is called for is when you're in the middle of an activity and suddenly get an idea about something else you want to do. If you're afraid you'll forget the idea, you may simply follow your nose from activity *A* to activity *B* to activities *C, D,* and *E,* leaving out a lot of stuff from unfinished activities along the way, which then becomes clutter. Along with a mess, you'll also be left, at the end of the day, with the dissatisfaction of having finished nothing you intended to do. The way to avert this pattern is to write the idea down as soon as the light bulb flashes, and then go on with what you're doing. So as not to interrupt the flow of your present activity, write the idea on anything you can find. Then, when you've finished the task at hand, transfer it into your planner or PDA and throw the piece of paper away, preferably setting a date for acting on the idea.

To increase the likelihood of your writing things down, carry writing materials with you—pens or pencils and three-by-five-inch cards or small memo pads—and/or keep small pads of paper and pens in every room. When I'm unusually busy I sometimes put a memo pad on a chain and hang it around my neck. It might look funny, but it works. Don't be discouraged about not having a perfect memory. Even computers need extra "memory" sometimes!

24. SWEEP AND VACUUM AT LEAST ONCE A WEEK.

How can I do that?" you protest. "Do you realize how long it's been since I've seen the floor? It's covered with CLUTTER!"

Yes, I know. But I said *once a week,* which means you have exactly one week to uncover enough floor to do a reasonable amount of sweeping and vacuuming. Which is exactly why I'm suggesting you pick an S & V day and stick to it no matter what. If there's only one square foot of floor visible, then clean that one square foot and tell yourself next week there'll be two square feet. Or, better yet, move some stuff and do more. The hope is that knowing you're going to S & V no matter what will have the same effect on you as knowing a friend is going to visit. A little extra motivation can't hurt.

Once your floor is mostly clear of clutter, cleaning it can be a satisfying experience. Be sure you have good equipment. Throw away the old broom with fuzz-balls stuck in the bristles and buy yourself a state-of-the-art broom and dust pan. Should you be inspired to mop a floor after you sweep it, you'll need a sponge mop that wrings out easily, a bucket, and the right kind of floor cleaner for the type of surface. For carpets, choose a vacuum cleaner that you can move around easily and that has attachments for getting under beds and knocking down cobwebs. Vacuuming is good exercise and will speed up your heart if you throw yourself into it.

Armed with the right equipment, set to work. Be systematic in covering the area—don't just sweep at random, but start at one end and clean each area thoroughly before going onto the next. Once a month, use the vacuum attachments to go under beds and along walls and cracks. The rest of the time it's OK to sweep around everything. Life is too short to spend *too much* time sweeping and vacuuming.

One further piece of advice: Be kind to your vacuum cleaner so it will be kind to you. Vacuum cleaners have a way of balking when you force them to eat hard little Things that give them indigestion. If it's been a long time since you swept an area, chances are it's littered with plenty of hard little Things. Use a broom and "deep-dish" snow shovel to scoop up the objects from the carpeted floor, then dump the contents into a box and sort them when you're finished. Or, if you'd rather, spend some time on your hands and knees picking up doodads before you vaccuum. It's great exercise, and who knows what gems you might find?

25. CHOOSE WHILE YOU'RE STILL IN THE STORE.

Part of living clutter-free is rethinking the way you shop in order to stem the tide of Things flowing into your space. One aspect of shopping is decision-making. If you're one of those people who can only choose if someone points a gun at your head, this can cause problems when you shop. Anytime you're torn between buying this Thing or that Thing, you may be tempted to buy them both rather than choose one and leave the other in the store. Maybe you even buy more than two rather than choose. Financial anxieties might provide you with the requisite gun to the head that forces you to choose, but if not you might choose not to choose as the easiest way out. The result is more stuff in your space that you probably won't use, a less user-friendly environment, and less freedom from clutter.

So let's imagine. You're standing there with a blue whatsit and a green whatsit, debating the virtues of each. The blue one goes with your eyes, but green is your favorite color. If you buy the blue one, you'll wish you had the green one, and if you buy the green one, you'll wish you had the blue one. You won't enjoy the whatsit you bought because you'll be so mad at yourself for not buying the other one. Either way you lose.

True. Choice always involves loss of what you don't choose. But you've probably endured far worse losses by now and survived. And why frame the decision as a lose-lose situation? Is your cup half empty or what? If you buy the blue whatsit, you gain the one that goes with your eyes. If you buy the green one, you get the one that's your favorite color. Either way you win.

Along with reframing a lose-lose decision as a win-win, take a step back and reflect on the consequences of past shopping decisions, especially when you were young and may have made some of the shopping mistakes we all make when we're learning. Did you get teased in adolescence for wearing the wrong tennis shoes? Did your parents get upset with you for buying something they considered inappropriate? Reconsidering the roots of shopping paralysis may help to alleviate it.

Decision-making involves using the highest nonreptilian centers of the brain and that consequently takes energy. When energy is down, the first thing people do is stop making decisions and let events take their course. If your energy is flagging, that's a bad time to shop. Next time you're shopping and you're about to take it all home with you rather than choose, muster up your energy by jogging up and down the escalator a few times. Then remind yourself of what you have to gain by choosing one whatsit over the other, which is not just the favored whatsit but a little more sense of control over your own destiny—and a little less clutter.

26. LET THE PHONE RING.

Are you a phone slave? Some people are as conditioned to jump when the phone rings as Pavlov's dog was conditioned to salivate at the sound of a bell. Living this way plays havoc with your ability to accomplish goals, including organizing. As a professional organizer, I've sometimes been taken aback when clients chose to spend half an hour of time for which they were paying me talking on the telephone while I sat waiting. *That's* conditioning.

The answering machine is a marvelous invention. Using it appropriately allows you to take charge of your time and accomplish what you want to accomplish. Of course, there are occasions when you may consciously choose to answer the phone—using a caller ID will help you decide—but if you routinely bypass the higher, decision-making centers of your brain by responding to a bell or a beep on a knee-jerk level, clutter—along with a lot other problems—is likely to result. Answering the phone in the midst of an activity raises the probability that you'll leave something out and never get back to it, and answering it during a de-cluttering session lowers the probability that you'll finish the job.

Training yourself to let the phone ring is not easy. Start by logging in all the calls you receive for three days and noting down the length of time you spent on each call. Then put a plus mark next to all the calls from people who had something to offer that you wanted—either business or personal—and a minus next to all the calls from people who wanted something from you. Include strangers who wanted to collect for charities or sell you something as well as "friends" seeking free therapy and family members making demands. At the end of the three days compare the numbers and decide if it's in your best interests to answer the phone when it rings.

Every time you receive a call, ask yourself, "Am I expecting a call that is important to *me?*" (Not someone else—you!) If the answer is no, let the phone ring. If you have trouble going cold turkey, disconnect the phone while you're working or wean yourself by allowing the phone to ring one more time each day before you answer. Pay attention to your feelings. What thoughts and fears go through your head as the ringing goes on? Talk back to negative automatic thoughts and face your fears.

If you don't have an answering machine, you still don't have to be a phone slave. Lacking such devices, you may choose to answer the phone more, but you'll need to perfect the art of ending calls quickly. Tell the person up front how much time you have for the call, or set a time to call him or her back. When a telemarketer calls, politely say you're not interested and, if the person keeps talking, hang up. Better yet, log onto www.donotcall.gov and make it illegal for telemarketers to call you.

Letting the phone ring is about setting boundaries. Practice setting boundaries with the phone, and you may end up setting other boundaries more effectively as well, including reducing your clutter piles. After all, both involve defining your priorities and sticking to them.

27. PRACTICE THE ART OF SYSTEMATIC SCANNING.

When you live with clutter every day, you may reach a point where you don't see it anymore. The psychological term for this is "accommodation." Systematic scanning—I'm talking about a mental process, not computer scanning—can help.

Scanning means searching your environment for something in particular. First you must decide what you're scanning *for*. You may be looking for your jacket, for example, and scan the room until your eyes rest on it. Or you scan the room for any article of clothing in order to collect clothes to put in the laundry basket. Vision, as Jean Piaget's research shows, is an active process. Even infants are constantly making choices about where to focus their eyes. To see everything all of the time is impossible. Scanning makes use of your freedom to see what you choose to see while ignoring the rest.

Scanning comes more naturally to some folks than to others. Some people's eyes are constantly darting here and there, taking in details. Others observe the environment more globally, which enables them to catch the "big picture" that natural scanners miss. If you're naturally a big-picture person, the practice of systematic scanning may help you to feel less overwhelmed and approach the problem of big clutter in a more organized fashion.

To scan a room systematically, decide what you're looking for— trouble spots, a particular kind of item such as clothes, papers, or books, or a certain object you want to find. Stand in the doorway of the room. Move your eyes slowly along each wall, starting on your left and ending up on your right. As your eyes move along the walls, keep reminding yourself of what you want them to take in. Then scan the floor in quadrants, keeping the object of your search in mind. If you have trouble staying focused, try looking through a cardboard tube or the lens of a camera. Or take scanning videos, zeroing in on target objects. When you watch films and videos, notice how directors do this.

As you begin to develop your systematic scanning skills, you can use them in several different circumstances:

- Scan a room as part of a "tour," looking for pockets of clutter that need to be addressed.

- Scan your whole home for a particular category of object and deal with all objects of that category at once: do a book scan, then purge and organize your books; do a paper scan and box up all the loose papers; do a clothing scan and get the clothes moving through the laundry cycle.

- Scan your space for a lost object. Approaching the search systematically may help you to find things you would otherwise have missed.

28. PUT UP PICTURES *NOW.*

Do you have pictures, all framed and ready to go, that have been leaning up against walls for years? What's kept you from hanging them? Are they pictures that you really don't like? If so, put them in your share box (see #54) and start thinking about buying something more to your taste.

If you *do* like the pictures, what's been holding you back? Is there a feeling that you can't hang the pictures in a room until it's clutter-free— that this should be the finishing touch to a room that's become a work of art itself? Are you afraid of hammering your thumb or knocking a hole in the plaster when you try to put the hooks up? Are you reluctant to commit to a spot for the pictures?

Whatever the hesitation, it's time to take action. While it might seem logical to think of putting up pictures as a reward for completing the drudgery of de-cluttering, not having pictures on the wall can make it more difficult to get on with the job. In order to de-clutter a room, you need to be able to enjoy being in the room, and bare walls don't help. Hanging pictures will make the room a place where you'll want to spend more time, which will put you in a position to de-clutter it. You may also feel more motivated to keep the room clutter-free so as not to spoil the effect of the art.

If dealing with a hammer and nails is scary for you, you can ask a more experienced handyperson to coach you through the picture-hanging process. Allow the person to help with adjusting heights, as two pairs of hands and eyes makes this easier, but don't let the person do the job for you. You don't want to miss the surge of power you'll feel when you succeed at a job you thought you couldn't do.

29. DO A LOOSE-PAPER HUNT.

When I begin working with new organizing clients, often they have papers strewn throughout their entire home, with no apparent logic as to which papers ended up where. In order to cut through the confusion and attack the paper problem head-on, my first recommendation to most clients is that we go around and gather up all the loose papers—those not already in files or boxes—so we can begin to make sense out of them and find them proper homes. I call this a loose-paper hunt, and it's a good thing to repeat from time to time.

To do a loose-paper hunt, you'll need some bankers' boxes and a felt-tipped marker. Put a box together and take it into the room where you have the most loose papers. Toss all the loose papers you find into the box. Important: *Do not look at the papers as you put them into the box. Do not put anything besides papers in the box.* From there, progress from room to room until Box #1 is full. Put the lid on the box. If you feel anxious, take a deep breath and tell yourself that the papers haven't gone down through a false bottom into a black hole beneath the box: they're still in there.

On the side of the box, write the names of the rooms from which you collected papers, with the first room entered at the bottom, the second room above it, and so forth. This gives you a "map" of the contents and where they came from (which is not necessarily where they will end up). Construct a second box and pick up where you left off with Box #2. Continue until you've collected all the loose papers in the house. If there are only a few, you may just have one box of papers to sort. If you have a lot of papers, you'll have a whole row of boxes. Line these up neatly next to a cleared sorting desk with #1 closest to the desk. Then sit down, open the first box, and begin sorting the papers using your favorite system (see #59).

30. RATE YOUR MEMORABILIA.

One of the reasons we keep Things is to serve as reminders of the past. Alas, for some of us, the reminders crowd out the present, clogging up our space and, ironically, losing their meaning due to overcrowding and underappreciation. Systematically rating your memorabilia may help you to gradually let go of those items that have little meaning for you so that you can more easily find and enjoy the ones that are particularly precious.

Go to an office supply store and buy several packages of self-sticking dots in different colors. Do a memorabilia scan throughout your home. Each time you come to a memorabilia object, stick a dot on it. If it's an item of great personal meaning to you—an item you'd try to rescue in a fire—use a red dot. If it's not that precious to you, but you like the item and/or frequently use it, give it a yellow dot. If you feel nothing at all when you look at the object and rarely use it, a green dot. If you feel angry, bitter, or hurt when you look at the item, use a blue dot.

Now take four boxes and label each with a dot of a corresponding color. Use these boxes to sort memorabilia papers and smaller items. Some of your old greeting cards, for example, make you feel wonderful to look at and go in the red-dot box. Others make you feel less wonderful but are pretty enough to still give you some pleasure and belong in the yellow-dot box. The green-dot box is for the cards that leave you cold, usually from people you barely know, or ones bearing just a signature. The blue box is for the birthday card that made you feel old, or the card sent with flowers when someone broke up with you.

When you've finished rating all your memorabilia, let them be.

You've accomplished the first stage of letting go, which is differentiation. Wait two weeks, then dispose of the green-dot Things, those about which you feel little or nothing. These will be the easiest to let go. Wait two more weeks, and get rid of the blue-dot objects, the icky reminders. Take them out on trash day and watch the truck drive them away, along with the anger and bitterness and pain. Then go inside, take off the red and yellow dots, and enjoy your memorabilia. Display or store the items. If necessary, take steps to preserve them. Most of all, feel their comfort and value, which will be all the richer because you've examined your feelings, and saved only what you truly want and need.

31. KEEP A PHONE LOG.

Is your household sprinkled with slips of paper on which are written names, phone numbers, and notes from answering machine messages? If so, start a phone log. A habit of logging in all significant incoming and outgoing calls (you don't have to log in recorded messages offering you a free trip to Las Vegas) not only eliminates message clutter but also enables you to communicate more effectively with others.

You can keep your phone log in a special notebook or in the "Daily Record of Events" pages of your planner. Use a new page for each day. If you're not using a planner, write the day of the week and the date at the top. Beneath it, put the type of call (VM = voice message; IN = incoming; OUT = outgoing), time, person's name, phone number, and notes on the content. In the left-hand margin next to each VM entry, put a small box in which you can make a check mark after you've returned a call or otherwise dealt with it. For example:

WEDNESDAY, MAY 15, 2004

- ☐ 9:21 VM: Deborah, nurse from Dr. Wallentine's office, 734-764-3245. Returned my call re ear problem.

- • 9:40 OUT: Deborah. Decided to try drops for two days, call back for appt. if not better.

- • 10:15 IN: Martin P. re contract, 212-904-3219. Final copy on its way.

- ☐ 12:05 VM: Esther re teaching schedule, 248-996-7145. Call her back to give preferences.

If you have only one phone in your home, this is easy. You just keep your log next to the phone. It becomes more complicated, however, when you have multiple phones. Rather than keep multiple logs, keep notepads next to each phone and use them for incoming calls only. Record the information, then transfer it into your log and dispose of the slip of paper. Try to use only one phone, the one where you keep your log, to listen for voice messages and make outgoing calls. If more than one person in your home answers the phone, leave pads of office-style message forms with carbons by each phone and set up a message board where household members can tack up messages for one another.

Although keeping a phone log takes effort, especially when you're getting the habit established, those who've managed to do so claim that it's changed their lives. Try it!

32. FIND A CLUTTER MATE.

Believe it or not, you're not the only one in the world who feels overwhelmed by Things. On the contrary, this planet is chock-full of individuals wringing their hands over clutter piles. Somewhere out there is someone who would love to be your clutter mate.

Joining forces with a clutter mate can be beneficial to both parties. For one thing, a major stumbling block to getting organized is the shame people sometimes feel about being disorganized. Shame thrives on solitude, and two people supporting each other cut their shame in half. For another, a clutter mate might have some great ideas that he or she would be willing to share.

If you're going to find a partner in de-cluttering, it's important to find the right one. It's best that your clutter mate begin with about the same level of chaos as you have in your own space. You'll need to feel comfortable with the person and feel that you can trust him or her to accept you as you are. A critical clutter mate will do more harm than good; an empathic clutter mate can make all the difference.

Where to find such a person? One possible source is your own family and friends. Several co-authors of organizing books are sisters or friends who became clutter mates. Another way to find a clutter mate is through a clutter support group. A few organizers run groups, and there are also twelve-step groups such as Clutterers Anonymous and Messies Anonymous (www.messies.com). If you work with an organizer, he or she may be willing to pair you up with another client. Also, going to a workshop on organizing or clutter control may give you a chance to team up with someone. In my own workshops, I always encourage participants to exchange phone numbers and keep in touch after the workshop is over.

Before the two of you have committed to being clutter mates, you should each tour the other person's space. Then sit down and talk about your goals. Decide how you're going to accomplish them and arrange regular meetings and check-ins. E-mail and voice mail can be great ways to communicate. As much as possible, try to alternate meetings in each other's space. You can pick a particular project, perhaps choosing one item from this book, that you will each work on that week. For example, you might both decide to work on keeping laundry moving for a week and compare notes.

As in any close relationship, there will be times when you and your clutter mate will be at odds with one another, but it's worth the effort to try to make the arrangement work. Use "I" statements to be clear with your clutter mate about what you need—or don't need. For example, "I need you to help me stay on track" or "I'd rather you didn't tell me to get rid of things." If all you want is support and you don't want suggestions, say so. Both of you need to agree to respect one another's possession boundaries and refrain from criticism. If the partnership works, you'll both gain tremendously—and de-cluttering will be just the beginning.

33. HOW DOES IT FEEL TO BE ACTIVE?

Are you the sort of person who's usually in motion or the sort who's usually still? Which state do you prefer? Many clutter-bound people seem to have a natural aversion to action. Lying in bed or sitting in a chair is their position of choice. When they're forced to be more active, they can't wait to be still again. Moving under their own power is unsettling, annoying, exhausting, even painful. Because they hate moving they don't, and the clutter piles up. These people often believe themselves to be lazy and find it liberating when I explain how biologically and environmentally complex the true causes of physical inertness can be.

If action doesn't feel good to you, it's helpful to try to figure out why (see *Making Peace with the Things in Your Life* for more), but for our purposes, just recognizing that action doesn't feel good is half the battle. Once you're aware of your aversion to action, you can take it into account in strategizing to keep your life clutter-free. Obviously, it's more important for you than for others to have a user-friendly environment and to get help from others. For the sake of your health as well as your environment, however, you'll need to challenge yourself to try to raise your tolerance for activity.

The key is to take baby steps. Start with tasks requiring only small muscle movements such as sorting papers or photos, and work your way up to more physically daunting tasks such as cleaning out basements and garages. Make lists of your routine tasks (see #6) and rank the tasks on each daily, weekly, monthly, and yearly list according to how much action is involved. Doing dishes, for example, is usually less physically taxing than doing laundry, which often involves carrying big loads and climbing stairs. Deal with to-do lists of nonroutine tasks the same way, working your way up from least to most physically challenging. While you're "conditioning," try to get help from others in doing tasks you're not yet ready to do. If some sort of physical disability is involved, be realistic about what's likely to ever be comfortable and make arrangements accordingly.

Freedom from clutter is not something you can achieve purely with your mind. A more clutter-free life is, by necessity, also a more active life. As you begin to see—and feel—the benefits of raising your tolerance for action, your aversion will diminish until you're actually able to enjoy pitching in. When that happens, you'll be on the road not only to clutter freedom but also to better health.

34. DIVIDE AND SUBDIVIDE.

When I was in grade school and went to camp, the "clean plate club" was the rule. I had no problem with it except when they served oatmeal, which I hated. I would always say, "No, thank you," but the counselors insisted that I eat at least a small scoop of the awful stuff. While every other camper at the table gobbled her cereal down so as to move on to cinnamon toast, I would first halve, then quarter, then eighth, then further dissect the dish of oatmeal down to individual grains. These I was able—just barely—to get down without gagging.

Thus I learned about dividing and subdividing, and it has served me well in performing unpleasant tasks throughout my life. Anytime a job seems overwhelming, I break it down into parts, and if the parts seem overwhelming, I break them down into even smaller parts.

Suppose the job you hate is purging files. If the thought of purging all the files in your cabinet makes you nauseous, downscale your goal to purging just one drawer. If purging one drawer seems unbearable, try half a drawer. If you can't stand half a drawer, try one hanging folder. If one hanging folder is too much, try one file folder. If one file folder is too much, focus on one sheet of paper. At some point the size of the job will be manageable. Or imagine your goal is to clean out your dirty attic. If it's too much to do all at once, how about just going through one box of books or a single trunk filled with clothes? If that's too much, could you do half a box or half a trunk?

When people don't divide and subdivide, their tasks can seem so daunting that they tend to walk away from clutter without doing anything about it. Now that you know this trick, you won't have to.

35. PURGE DEEP STORAGE
AREAS FIRST.

When your basement, attic, or storage bins are already filled to capacity, you begin to store items in your living space as well. This makes clutter-free living impossible. Over time, as new items flow into your space, stored possessions take over more and more of your household. Often the first area to go is the garage. Soon there's no more room in it for cars. Then boxes begin piling up in the bedrooms. An extra bathroom may become a storage closet. Eventually, even corners in the living room are filled. Once this starts happening, the optimal solution is to strike at the root of the problem by purging legitimate storage space and thus creating the space you need to store items kept in areas meant for other purposes.

Chances are, if an object is already in a standard storage area, you value it less than if it's in your living room. If you have to get rid of some Things, it's best to start with those in deep storage to make room for those in surface storage. This means playing fruit basket upset until you're using more of your home for living than for squirreling away excess items. It does not mean making your deep-storage space perfect: your goal is simply to create more room for Things that are currently stored in your living space.

Not that storage doesn't have a purpose. Some stored Things are used only seasonally. Others represent pieces of family history or precious memories that you feel obligated to preserve for your heirs. Still others may serve you in an emergency, or an adventure on which you're planning to embark, or in a future stage of life in which your needs will be different. These items need to be stored. What you don't need to keep are items that are just "there." Get the Things out that mean nothing to you and that you never use, and make room for objects that have a legitimate place in storage.

Before you start purging your deep-storage areas, research charities and resale shops and decide where you'll take the Things you purge. If you find it difficult to let go of items, look for a supportive friend or family member to go through them with you, or hire a professional organizer. If you need to wean yourself by doing this in stages, that's OK.

Purge everything you can and consolidate the rest. Remind yourself that the more you take out, the more you'll be able to clear out your living space and live clutter-free. Sweep the floor, wipe off shelves, and consider adding new shelves and containers. Then, when you start to move surface storage items into deep storage, purge out useless items from your living space as well. Ideally, by the time you're finished, you'll have empty shelves left in your deep-storage areas for future needs and nothing at all stored inappropriately in your living areas.

36. USE PLEASURES AS
REWARDS, NOT ESCAPES.

Personally, I'm not a puritan. I believe pleasure is a good thing, as long as it doesn't hurt anyone, including yourself. If you love reading romance novels but want to live clutter-free, then by all means read them—but only after you've done your daily chores. Use them as a reward, not to escape from the clutter dragon.

Reading romances, sci-fi, mysteries, fantasy, self-help, classics, newspapers, magazines, or whatever else you enjoy is only one possible pleasure that can serve as either an escape from daily chores or a reward for staying clutter-free. There's also television, videos, DVDs, Internet, sleep, aerobics, work, music, shopping, water-skiing, golf, tennis, basketball, horseback riding, chess, crossword puzzles, jigsaw puzzles, computer games, video games, model railroads, crafts, coin collecting, stamp collecting, paint-by-number pictures, and a host of other nontoxic, pleasurable activities in which human beings engage.

A lot of clutter happens because people use pleasures as escapes rather than as rewards. When you start doing this, it can turn your stuff—and your life—upside-down. Most of us have one or two pleasures that are a little too pleasurable. When we're engaged in them, we feel trapped by a magnetic force that refuses to let go. This has a way of playing havoc with schedules and surroundings. I, for one, have learned that I cannot watch part of a BBC video series of the *Upstairs, Downstairs* variety (our public library has a great collection) and be able to stop in the middle and get back to work. If I take one of these tapes home, I can forget about anything else I planned to do that day. But if I tell myself that when I'm done with my chores for the day, I can go get the next video or two from the library, I finish everything in nothing flat. The same pleasure that can be an addictive escape from constructive activity can also be an excellent motivator if you make a point of using it that way.

Make a list of your favorite pastimes. Do you use any of them as escapes rather than as rewards? Be honest with yourself. Is any escapist activity making your life unmanageable? In that case, you may need to rethink your use of it, or even consider foregoing it altogether. At the same time, be sure you don't demand so much of yourself that there's no reward time left. Without the motivating power of pleasurable rewards, you're likely to become resistant to working toward clutter freedom at all—and that's when you'll really feel compelled to use rewards as escapes.

37. MAKE USE OF THE SNOWBALL EFFECT.

When you don't have much energy, it often seems best to conserve it by doing as little as possible. The assumption is that biological energy works like the energy produced by coal or oil, but this is not the case. While conservation of fossil fuels may be adaptive, when it comes to human energy, the more you use, the more you have.

Suppose it's Saturday morning and your kitchen is in chaos. You're feeling tired, so you decide to just deal with the unwashed dishes. Once the dishwasher is humming away and the pots and pans are sparkling in the rack, you feel a little more energetic and decide to wipe off the countertops. As you do so, you notice that the food processor looks a little scummy and take a scouring pad to it. Before you know it, you've cleaned off all the appliances on the counter. The oven sure could use a cleaning. By mid-morning, you know you should stop and do some errands, but you can't. You tell yourself you'll stop when you've finished alphabetizing all your spices, but when you do finish you notice that the light fixture is filled with insects and you set up a ladder. At the end of the day, you've cleaned out all the kitchen cupboards, your kitchen is organized and spotless, and you're starting to think about the dining room.

How does this happen? When the snowball effect occurs, each task you complete gives you a little more energy as you become increasingly focused on moving forward toward a goal. Biologically, the reasons are complex and may involve hormones, neurotransmitters, and your overall physical state as well. Psychologically, such momentum may develop into the kind of optimal experience that Mihalyi Czikszentmihalyi calls "flow."

Some people may experience the snowball effect more than others.

If it doesn't happen for you, then don't try to force it, but if it does, plan accordingly and make use of it. Instead of forcing yourself to stop at the end of your regulation two-hour work session, go with the snowball effect and you'll end up doing more than you ever thought you could.

38. IS IT WORTH IT?

When people try to hang on to too much stuff, it's often because they fail to ask an important question at key moments: Is it worth it? When you develop a habit of asking this question, you may begin to realize that you're paying a far higher price for some of your Things than they're really worth to you.

This may be true even monetarily. The price of owning any given item extends beyond what it costs to buy it. There's also the cost of housing it, cleaning it, protecting it, and maintaining it. But the financial cost is only the beginning.

Things also cost you time. Before you start clipping three thousand newspaper articles that you'll need to read and organize, ask yourself if the information you'll get from them is worth the hours of time you could have spent taking your kids to the park. What about the new trailer you bought in order to "get away from it all"—will the actual leisure you get be worth the hours of cleaning, stocking, driving, and maintaining the vehicle? How many hours do you spend dusting your five hundred sets of china dishes? If you spend ten minutes a day agonizing over what to do with the latest batch of junk mail, is it worth that kind of time?

And there's also the human cost. I never cease to be amazed at the extent to which people are willing to sacrifice relationships for the sake of material objects. One of my clients did not speak to her sister for years because when their mother died, the sister took an item of sentimental value without asking. Many marriages break up over material Things—wanting them, not being able to afford them, lavishing time and attention on them, being unable to part with them. Parents become enraged with one another and allow children to witness quarrels and even violence over a torn carpet or a broken washing machine. And meanwhile, on a mammoth scale throughout history, human beings have killed and maimed each other over all sorts of inanimate objects, in particular land—also known as "dirt." Is it worth it?

MAJOR!

39. BREAK THE CLIPPING HABIT.

Clipping articles from newspapers and magazines can be worth the effort under certain circumstances:

- If you're a student who has to write a report for school based on a clipping

- If you're making a collage

- If you wrote the article yourself, or the article is about you or someone you care about

- If you're an artist, composer, or creative writer who pastes clippings in your journal as possible material for a future work

- If you've set up topic files that you actually refer to for your hobbies or work

- If you want to send someone an article about a mutual friend

- If you're marooned on an island where there are no libraries and no connections to the Internet

The fact that something "seems interesting" is not enough a reason to clip it out and throw it into a pile. Lots of stories are interesting. But there's an endless tide of new stories coming your way in magazines and newspapers, and the Internet allows you to find virtually any information you need, when you need it.

In many cases, clipping is nothing more than a compulsion, born of fear: fear of being without that one piece of vital information; fear of your memory failing; fear of getting lost in the library stacks; fear of not having read everything under the sun. These are perfectly normal fears that we all feel at times, but they're not fears that you have to give in to.

Meanwhile, the clippings pile up. Fragile and oddly shaped, they wrinkle and tear and stick up out of file folders or crumble into bits and disappear into the carpet. If you really have to clip out articles, make a rule that you must file or mail them weekly or toss them out at the end of the week. Better yet, face your fears, and break the clipping habit altogether. You'll be glad you did.

40. GET A GREAT LETTER
OPENER.

I used to let mail pile up before opening it. Then, one December a classy gold-plated letter opener arrived as a gift. This transformed the experience of opening mail. Not only could I now slit envelopes with lightening speed, I also got to feel like Mrs. Vanderbilt opening replies to her garden party invitations. Now each day I can't wait to get my hands on more unopened envelopes.

Recently, I did a search on the Internet and was amazed at the diversity of available letter openers. These included brass, crystal, silver, stainless steel, gold-plated, jade, ivory, and wood letter openers, a Mount Vernon letter opener, a letter opener designed by Frank Lloyd Wright, a hand-carved zebra letter opener from Kenya, a dagger letter opener from Medieval Weapons Art, and a letter opener from the Freud Museum in London emblazoned with Dr. Sigmund's signature. Obviously, the one danger of shopping for a great letter opener is that you'll end up collecting them! Consider yourself warned.

My second cousin Sara claims that her life was changed by the purchase of an automatic letter opener. According to Sara, hand letter openers are nothing compared with the surgical zip of this "cutting edge" technology. One company I checked with advertises mechanical letter openers ranging from $32 to $8,373. (The $8,373 model can open 36,000 envelopes per hour—a perfect gift for those who are *extremely* popular.)

Maybe one of these days I'll listen to Sara and send for one of the automatic letter openers, but I'm in no hurry. I'm too busy opening envelopes and planning my next garden party.

41. MOVE FROM QUANTITY TO QUALITY.

In the late 1980s, my mother, then in her seventies, decided that she could no longer manage the three-bedroom ranch house she had lived in for almost thirty years. She did some research on retirement communities in Des Moines, Iowa, where she lived, and chose a two-bedroom apartment on the tenth floor of a luxurious high-rise. Before she moved into her new apartment, she hired an interior decorator to give her some suggestions. She also sorted through seventy-odd-years' worth of possessions, which included family heirlooms that had been passed down since the 1600s.

Of the many Things she owned, she kept only the finest, and of those, only what suited her new décor: the best furniture, the softest towels, the good set of china, her favorite books. The rest she sent on their way—to me or my brother, to other family members, to the library, the Goodwill, the historical museum. She also went shopping and bought some lovely new items that went with the things she kept.

When my mother finally moved into her new apartment, it was to a place that contained only her most cherished possessions and little else, a real showplace compared to the home she had left. Everything she owned had been distilled down to its essence like an expensive perfume. She had made the transition from quantity to quality.

This is a transition that many of us, old or young, would do well to make. Part of living clutter-free is consistently opting for quality over quantity in deciding what you keep and what you buy. Try this: Get together all the items you own of one type—all the vases in your house, for example. Then rank them according to quality. In doing this, don't just consider how valuable something is in monetary terms, but how much pleasure you derive from the object as well.

The clay vase your son made in grade school may merit a higher quality rating than the Waterford someone bought you in Ireland. Quality is whatever is most precious to you, regardless of price tag. Now separate the highest quality item from the others. Set it in the middle of a table by itself and admire it. Meditate on it for a moment or two, appreciating it from every angle. As you examine it apart from its inferior counterparts, you may be surprised by its radiance. Isn't it easier to enjoy it now that it's not lost in a crowd? Examine the other items and discard what you can.

If you have shopping to do, putting yourself in a "quality, not quantity" frame of mind will not necessarily save you money, but it will keep you from arriving home overloaded with Things you bought just because they were on sale and for which you'll now have to find homes. If your space is limited, thinking quality, not quantity can make the difference between living clutter-bound and clutter-free.

42. KEEP THE DISHES
MOVING ON.

If they're on the dining room table or somewhere else in the house, move them to the kitchen counters. If they're sitting dirty on the kitchen counters, scrape, rinse, and stack them. If they're scraped, rinsed, and stacked, put them into the sink or dishwasher. If they're in the sink or dishwasher, wash them and dry them. If they're washed and dried, put them away. Keep the dishes moving until they're stored away where they belong.

If your dishes are getting stuck somewhere in the cycle, do some troubleshooting. Where are the dishes piling up? What's going on when you put them there? Are you eating meals all over the house because your dining room table is too cluttered to use? Do the dishes stay on the table because you're always rushing off somewhere? Do they stay stacked by the sink because you feel that dishwashing is "woman's work," or you resent the fact that your brother never had to do dishes? Have you just been doing dishes so long you're bored sick with them?

If boredom is the problem, there are two possible routes to go: combining dishwashing with another, more interesting activity, or the Zen route of transforming dishwashing into a pleasurably mindful mediation exercise. If you want to combine dishwashing with another activity, choose something that uses your eyes, ears, and brain, but leaves your hands free: listen to music or a book tape, watch TV, talk with a friend, either in person or on a hands-free phone, sing, dance, recite poetry, or share the job with one of your kids. I grew up drying dishes while one of my parents washed. Although I claimed to hate this and begged them to get a dishwasher, I also had a lot of great conversations with each of them during this time.

Done mindfully, dishwashing becomes far more pleasant than

when done mindlessly or with dread. Approach the process slowly, step by step. To do this, you need to clarify the steps in your mind. The first is to clear the table. This means not only carrying all the used dishes into the kitchen, but removing placemats, napkins, tablecloths, candles, and centerpieces, cleaning off the surface of the table, and sweeping the area around it for crumbs.

Next, put all leftovers in containers and store them in the refrigerator. Then scrape leftovers off the dishes into a garbage pail or disposal, rinse each item under hot water, and stack the dishes next to the sink or load them into the dishwasher. Group them into four categories: glassware, pottery, silverware, and "pots and pans" (a category that includes utensils, mixing bowls, measuring cups, and everything else you used to prepare the meal).

If you're washing dishes by hand, fill the dishpan with water that's as hot as you can stand and pour in some dishwashing liquid. Wash the glassware first so it will get the hottest water, then the pottery, silverware, and pots and pans. Feel each piece for non-visible food residue. Rinse the dishes and let them dry in a drying rack, or dry them with a clean dishtowel. Put each item away as you dry it, or put items away before you start preparing the next meal, when you may need them.

If you use a dishwasher, the tricky part is to remember to empty it once the dishes have cooled down. Make a point of doing so at least once a day, drying any items that are still wet.

You may not always have time to finish the dishes before leaving home. If you have to rush off, at the very least, scrape, rinse, and stack the dishes after you use them. Food scraps left on unwashed dishes quickly become a breeding ground for bacteria, and they are much harder to clean. It's fine to leave rinsed dishes stacked next to the sink; when you get home you can pick up where you left off. Make it a rule never to leave unwashed dishes any longer than a day. Doing so will not only free you from dish clutter, it will also mean you'll have the tools and dishes you need to prepare the next meal.

43. DO A TRASH SCAN.

Are you or others in your household slow to throw out the trash? Do a trash scan before you take it out and free yourself from trash clutter. Begin at the front door and scan each wall, then look at each of the four quadrants of the floor for items that, in your mind, un-equivocally belong in the trash or recycle bins.

What constitutes "trash" is situational. If you're on a desert is-land, nothing is trash: you need everything to survive. If you're living out of a shopping cart, you might collect items that you would throw away if you had your own place. In doing your trash scan, don't worry about items that you're not sure about. Just gather up those items almost anyone would throw away or recycle. These include the following, among others:

- Used paper dishes, cups, and napkins

- Used tissues and toilet paper

- Used paper towels

- Used bandages and other medical waste (may require special disposal)

- Empty cans

- Empty bottles

- Cardboard tubes

- Broken rubber bands

- Empty packaging

- Empty envelopes

- Crumpled up newspapers

- Filthy rags

- Used dental floss

- Dead batteries (toxic—may require special recycling)

- Burned out light bulbs (wrap in newspaper or foam food container)

- Food scraps

- Pet feces

- Balls of hair or fuzz

- Broken and unfixable items

Finish your trash scan by taking what you've collected out to the dumpster, garbage can, or recycle bins. The sooner you get it out of your house, the better. Now take a look at all the nice, empty spaces you've quickly created.

A trash scan, done every day or two, can make a significant difference in the size of your clutter piles. Unless you have obsessive compulsive disorder, it involves no agonizing decisions. While it's not nice to label other people "trash," Things are not people, and their feelings aren't going to be hurt if you designate them for the recycle station or town dump. You're the one in charge here, and if a Thing is trash to you, then it's, well . . . trash.

44. LOOK INSIDE.

Are you afraid to put your papers in a closed filing cabinet for fear you'll never see them again? One possible solution is to use only open-topped containers. However, these are less convenient, as they take up more floor space unless you stack them, which defeats the purpose. Clear containers also make contents more visible, at least as a whole, but again, they don't generally stack like drawers in a filing cabinet. Another alternative is to use standard filing cabinets but commit to regularly looking inside of them until you know exactly where each paper belongs.

If you're afraid to use closed file drawers, it could be because of certain memory glitches that require special indexes as well as more perusal before you have a map in your head telling you where everything belongs. (Or it could be you simply don't trust that anything you can't see still exists. If that's the case, the way to build trust is now and then to open the drawers and reassure yourself that, yes, the papers you thought had disappeared down a black hole are, in fact, still there.)

To solidify your sense of where things are filed, spend some time in your office or study reading the index—if you haven't made one, do so—on the front of the top file drawer (see #23). Then open the drawer and look at the file folders inside each hanging folder. Look inside the individual folders if you get the urge. Review each drawer in the same way. Keep doing this review until you're sure you don't need to anymore. Once you know where papers belong, you'll be more likely to file new ones instead of using the top of your desk as a filing cabinet.

This strategy also can work for other closed containers such as dresser drawers, closets, or cardboard boxes—anything you can't easily see into (see #52). Spend a little time each week familiarizing yourself with the written index and physical contents of closed containers around your home, and it will pay off when you need to find something or can't decide where to put something new. The end result is less clutter.

45. MAKE A "TO SORT" BASKET.

Do you leave papers spread out all over your dining room table as a way of motivating yourself to sort them? Do you believe that if you force yourself and your family long enough to eat off TV trays instead of using the table, you'll finally succumb to this torture and clean up your act?

If this is your game, it's time to get real. What's going on? Why are these papers ending up on the table instead of in your office action system? Chances are, you're coming in too tired and rushed to take the papers into another room and sort them right away. Realistically, the situation is probably not going to change, and that's OK. It does not mean, however, that your unsorted papers have to keep the table perpetually buried. To prevent this from happening, put a "to sort" basket on the table and throw everything into it.

My "to sort" basket is rectangular, a little bigger than 8 1/2" by 11", painted green, with little handles at each end. I bought it at a hardware store and have loved it ever since. I have an identical but smaller basket next to it for outgoing mail. When mail comes in, I immediately put everything I can in the recycle bin. Anything I'm going to keep goes in the "to sort" basket. When I bring some instructions home from a medical appointment, or the bank teller gives me a brochure, or I get a receipt from the post office, the new item goes in the "to sort" basket. Every two or three days when I'm not too busy, and once a week when I am, I take the basket upstairs and sort the papers into our system, a set of cubbies in a desk-top sorter. If I were a different kind of person, I'd sort and file my papers as soon as they came in, but organizing isn't always my first priority. Sometimes I'd rather call someone up or get a snack, or flop down on the couch and look out at the birds. I'm human, and that's why I have a "to sort" basket.

46. ONE TYPE OF THING, ONE HOME.

It's easier to get yourself to put something away if you know exactly where it belongs. If you don't know, putting an object in its home means reviewing your entire mental map in order to decide on a new place for it. This takes a lot of time and mental energy. Once you know exactly where each Thing belongs and with what, the process of de-cluttering speeds up immensely.

When it comes to creating homes for Things, disorganized people have a way of becoming far too complicated. Their minds begin to branch and rebranch like the tributaries of the Mississippi delta. Soon you have six different places where you keep six different kinds of tape, for example. While this might enable you to store the various rolls of tape nearer where you use them—always a good thing to do—it can also make a muddle in your head as you struggle to remember whether the masking tape belongs in the desk drawer, the kitchen drawer, or the supply closet. If you know that all the rolls of tape in your house, regardless of type, are stored in a single plastic shoe box in your office supply closet (a "tape place"), it might require a little more walking, but it makes it a lot easier to remember both where to put any kind of tape and where to find it. If your home has several stories you might want to make a home on each floor for kinds of Things you use all the time such as scissors, tape, glue, or pens. The principle is the same.

The one home for each type of object need not be a single container, but it does need to be a recognizable part of a container. On a supply closet shelf, for example, you might have a pile of transparencies, a pile of label sheets, and a pile of legal tablets stored side by side. Each pile makes a distinct home for that item. Better yet, you might use one-third of a vertical sorter for each type of sheet or pad.

Once you've created a single home for a single type of Thing, you may want to use special strategies to help you remember where the home was. These include labels (see #52), indexes (see #23), maps, and databases.

47. ASSESS YOUR
INFORMATION NEEDS.

When it comes to collecting information, it's easy to get it backwards. A piece of information comes into your hands by chance that might be useful, so you keep it. By doing this, you play a purely reactive role, acting as nothing more than a gatekeeper for incoming information. This is a fast route to information overload. The more information you keep, the harder it is to organize. The solution is to think *proactively* about what information you really need for your present life.

Start by listing your various roles. For example:

- Family member

- Citizen

- Craft enthusiast

- Entrepreneur

Then consider what tasks you need to perform for each of these roles, and what information you need in order to perform each task. For example:

FAMILY MEMBER

- Pay bills

  - Checkbook

  - Bank statements

  - Bills

- Deal with family health issues
  - Medical records
  - Prescriptions
  - Health insurance forms and statements
  - Handouts from providers
  - Information on specific conditions: diabetes, colitis, sleep apnea
  - Appointment cards
- Manage children's education
  - Report cards
  - Schoolwork
  - School calendar
  - Teachers' phone numbers
- Maintain household
  - Information on cleaning, organizing, decorating, home repairs
  - Instructions for appliances
  - Phone numbers of repair people
  - Warrantees
  - Catalogs

You may want to break down the information categories further in some cases. Once you've typed out a list of the information you need to perform the tasks associated with your various roles, then go through your papers and find as much of that information as you can.

Check off each item on your list as you locate it. If there are information gaps, use the telephone, computer, or library to fill them. Anything that doesn't fit into your information categories is extraneous. It might still be interesting, and if you have the space for it, there's no reason you shouldn't keep it; if, on the other hand, space is at a premium, consider purging it.

Writing out information lists takes time, and you may choose to use your time some other way. But even if you don't list every bit of knowledge you need, just thinking about your information needs in a general way will help you to be more selective in dealing with the many papers that come at you every day.

48. POST REMINDERS.

We don't like to admit this to ourselves, but people are animals. Like all animals, we need more than one repetition of a reminder to do something before it becomes a habit. When you teach your dog to sit, you don't just say, "Sit, Rover," and expect him to sit every time you say it forever after. Likewise, when you want to train yourself—or your partner, your child, your student, your roommate, or whomever—to do something new, saying it just once is unlikely to bring about permanent change.

Posting reminders someplace highly visible provides the mind with the frequent repetitions needed to cultivate the habits needed to eliminate big clutter. If you're encouraging other people to change, this may help preserve the relationship during the difficult period of habit-changing by cutting down on the frequency of oral reminders, aka nagging. When you give oral reminders to intimates, you may be tempted to add a few extra words: "You *always* leave your shoes on the stairs. Don't you know this is dangerous? One of these days somebody is going to break their neck and it will be all your fault. Don't you ever think about anybody but yourself?" Instead of all that, how about a neat sign, posted in a strategic place:

PLEASE KEEP THE STAIRS CLUTTER-FREE AT ALL TIMES.
                                            THE MANAGEMENT

With which approach would you be most likely to comply?

Anything you can do to catch the eye will make a sign more effective. Post the sign where people are sure to see it. Print your message in large block letters. Use bright fluorescent colors, glitter, or pictures. Catchy phrases and humor will make it easier for others to remember your message.

The principle of sign-posting is no different when the only person you're trying to retrain is yourself. Putting up a sign for yourself can help stop the angry tapes in your head when you trip over the shoes you left on the stairs. Over time, the wall sign's message might end up posted in your head. Once that's happened, you can take the wall sign down. Mission accomplished.

49. PLAN YOUR WARDROBE.

Are you proactive or reactive in shopping for clothes? Some people simply wander through a department store and buy anything that strikes their fancy. When they get home, they find that nothing goes with anything else, so they have to go out and buy more clothes to match the ones they bought. They can also wind up with far more sweaters than they need and not nearly enough pants. Taking time to plan your wardrobe at the beginning of each season before you shop can help to eliminate those extra clothes packed into your closet that for one reason or another you never wear.

Start by looking at what you already have. Sort your clothes by type. Get rid of any garments that don't fit, look worn, or just make you feel ugly. Tell yourself that you deserve only the best. This doesn't mean you have to buy everything at Saks Fifth Avenue. Buying just the right sweater at the Salvation Army store is better than buying just anything from an exclusive department store. To quote a recent article by Zenita Wickham in *Balance* magazine:

> *Style is not religious devotion to the latest clothing or beauty trends. Style is not sold in malls or even expensive boutiques. In fact, style cannot be bought anywhere. Rather, style—a quality most find hard to define yet instantly recognizable—is created.*

Now that you've purged what you don't like, look at what's left. Make up as many outfits as you can from what you have. Are there garments you can mix and match? Is there something you like that doesn't currently go with anything? If so, put it in a bag or make a note of it on a list to take with you when you shop. Also consider how you're planning to spend your time during the next four months. Will you be wearing professional or casual clothes most of that time? Are you planning to take a trip someplace where your wardrobe needs will be different? Is a special occasion coming up that will require special clothes? How many garments of each type do you need? Make a list of items to be purchased and how many. For example:

2 sweaters

1 blazer

2 pairs pants

1 pair dress shoes

1 pair running shoes

Now comes the fun part. Look through some fashion magazines: Spend a little time window shopping without buying to get a feel for what's available. Then go back and look at what you have. What are your best colors? What styles tend to look good on you? To what extent do your clothes express who you are? Do you wear classic styles to please someone else when at heart you're a bohemian?

Once you've considered how many items you need and have a general idea of what colors and styles you favor, you're ready to hit the stores. If you'd like more shopping help than family and friends can provide, consider hiring a wardrobe consultant, or make an appointment with a personal shopper—a free service—at any large department store.

Shopping is not the only aspect of planning your wardrobe seasonally; the other aspect is storage. As each season begins, you may want to put the clothes you're unlikely to wear in storage—sleeveless tops in the winter, heavy sweaters in the summer, for example—and get those out that suit the months to come. Decide which stored items you'll keep and do whatever washing, ironing, mending, altering, or dry-cleaning needed to make them as good as new. Store the out-of-season garments in plastic zipper-bags with cedar-wood rings around the hangers to protect them from moths, place them in a cedar chest, or—if your space is limited, pack them into empty suitcases with cedar blocks. Line the in-season ones up in your closet by type to make them easier to find, preferably on sturdy, uniform hangers.

As an organizer, I've learned that when clients begin to plan their wardrobes, they end up with far fewer clothes in their closets than when they purchase garments impulsively. Initially, they may buy some new outfits, adding to their stock, but this enables them to get rid of many more old outfits that they now realize don't fit their personal style or match their other belongings. It's about taking charge of your clothes and your life.

50. BREAK THE TACTILE
CONNECTION.

A key concept when it comes to letting go of Things is emotional bonding. Touch plays a major role where bonding is concerned. When a mother first holds a newborn infant, she becomes instantly attached to that child, which is why mothers whose infants are to be put up for adoption often choose not to hold their babies.

Although it might seem silly, people can also become extremely bonded to material objects—and not just to teddy bears. Given the importance of touching to attachment, picking up an item—especially if it's soft and fuzzy, but even if it's not—is likely to make you want to hang on to it. If you want to break your bond with an object and pass it on to someone else, one trick is to let someone else do the touching.

Your helper needs to know that his or her role is *only* to physically handle the object. You are to make all the decisions yourself about what to keep and what to dispose of. This might sometimes frustrate your helper, who might be tempted to challenge your decisions. But if you allow the helper to take total control and make decisions for you, you'll end up feeling violated and resentful and may hang on to things to try to regain control. Choose a helper whom you can trust to respect your autonomy and explain the limits of his or her role in the process. Issue reminders as needed.

Even if you're working without a helper, it's important to keep the tactile connection in mind and do what you can to minimize touching. Try wearing work gloves, using pick-up tools, or leaving items in boxes rather than handling them with your naked hands. It just might make letting go a little easier.

51. SAY ANYTHING BUT "YES."

Many organizing clients with whom I've worked have been automatic yes-sayers. Overall, this is not a bad way to live. Those who go through life saying nothing but "no" miss out on a lot. People who greet the world with arms wide open have a lot of interesting experiences along the way. Alas, they also tend to collect clutter.

I'm not suggesting that you should become a recluse with a "keep out" sign on your door, but there are times when a judiciously chosen alternative to "yes" has the power to dramatically reduce the amount of clutter in your life. Note that you don't necessarily need to say "no" straight out. If you find it hard to verbalize the N-word, start with "not now," "maybe sometime," "later," "I wish I could," or another soft negative. In many social circles, people will read between the lines, and you can work your way up to being more direct with those who don't. For now, what matters is to modify the "come one, come all" response that has gotten you into trouble. That means cutting down on the proportion of "yes" to "no" responses to others' demands as well as your own.

In certain situations in particular, an impulsive "yes" is likely to open the floodgate to clutter:

- When someone asks you to commit to some sort of time-consuming activity, reducing the number of hours, minutes, and seconds available for keeping your space more clutter-free

- When a cluttery person who has no intention of changing his or her habits asks to move in with you

- When someone offers you space-occupying Things you don't want or need

- When someone asks you to accompany him or her on a shopping spree, particularly to a shopping mall or large discount store

- When you get a sudden urge to do something else while in the midst of clutter-reducing chores

If you've been saying "yes" all your life, the habit won't be easy to break. Two strategies can help: First, get a big jar and fill it with marbles. Get another jar and leave it empty. Every time you say anything but "yes," move a marble from the full jar to the empty, non-yes jar. When the non-yes jar is full, give yourself a reward. (Decide ahead of time what that will be.) Second, get support from others. Explain to your cheering section what you're trying to do and ask them to whoop and clap whenever you report saying anything but yes.

As you begin to change your ways, you can expect some unpleasant feelings. You might feel guilty about all the people you're no longer saving—or trying to save—from disasters. You might feel anxious about missing out on the experience of a lifetime. You might feel sad that life is short and time is fleeting. These feelings are normal. Don't try to escape them by going back to saying "yes." Instead, vent your feelings to someone empathic and counter them with self-talk: They too shall pass.

Above all, don't take yourself to task if you slip back into old habits now and then. Just resolve that at the next opportunity, you'll say anything but yes.

52. LABEL IT SO YOU CAN READ IT.

Labels are a powerful organizing tool. If we all had perfect memories, they wouldn't be necessary, but most of us don't. If you create a home for a Thing and then don't label the home and don't put the object away right after you use it, there's a good chance you'll forget where that home is and put the object away in a different home, then another, and another. The poor homeless Thing floats around and never really settles down anywhere. If this happens to a lot of your possessions, every time you clean up you'll have to create a lot of new homes. This takes thought and effort, which is often tempting to avoid, so you don't clean up and clutter results. Hence, the need for labels. Once you've labeled an object's home, putting it away becomes a lot easier, and the pattern is reversed.

Labels can take many different forms. What matters most is that you be able to read them. Legibility is especially important in the case of filing. A major reason people can't find papers in folders is that the labels on them are too hard to read. Labels printed on a computer or label maker are terrific, especially if you use big bold caps, but it also works fine to make labels in big block letters with a medium-point, felt-tipped pen. After you've finished labelling folders, label each drawer on the outside with an index of its contents (see #23).

Another situation in which labels are essential is when using cardboard boxes in the midst of a de-cluttering job. If you don't label the sorting boxes as you go during a work session, you won't know what's in the boxes when you come back to them and will have to start all over. Knowing that you don't know what's in the boxes may keep you from coming back to them. In this way, the process breaks down, all for the want of a label.

Storage boxes should be labeled with a thick, nonsmelly marker in a place where the labels are easiest to read. Color coding can make labels easier to see, or you might prefer labelling with pictures instead of words. Draw a picture of a shoe on the outside of a box containing shoes, for example. Using humor or emotional language on labels can also increase visibility. "Oddball Dishes" or "Smelly Old Socks" works better than just "Dishes" or "Socks," for example. In the end, if you know where things go, you're more likely to put them away, and labels truly help.

53. TUCK IT IN.

Do papers flop up over the tops of your file folders? Do your sheets hang down below the blankets on the bed? Is a sock hanging out of your bureau drawer? One quick clutter-reduction strategy is to go around and tuck Things in.

Some people seem to have been born tucking. As toddlers, they probably tucked their shirts into their diapers. Other people never develop the tucking habit. Where clothes are concerned, tucking tops into bottoms is no longer a fashion requirement, but with papers and other nonwearable possessions, tucking in is still cool.

Why, then, doesn't everyone tuck? In the case of papers, accommodation (getting used to it) and being more auditory than visual in the way you experience the world seem to be important factors. Often I've worked with clients who appeared totally oblivious to papers sticking every which way out of files. Likewise with clothes hanging out of drawers. Some people who fail to tuck, however, may also be rebelling against a voice in their head that screams, "Tuck that in, you slob!" They forget that they're spoiling work that *they* did themselves.

To raise your awareness of the tucking issue, walk around your home and do a tucking scan. Each time you see something untucked, deal with any rebellious feelings you may have and tuck it in. Then step back and take in the new, tucked look.

One word of warning: There is a difference between tucking and stashing. Some people consistently tuck everything away into drawers and cupboards, which become pockets of hidden clutter. When you tuck something away, be sure that what you can't see from the outside is as neat as what you can see.

54. MAKE A SHARE LIST.

When people have trouble getting rid of Things, it's not always because they're emotionally unable to let go of them. It can also be because they don't have a clear idea of where they should dispose of something. Some folks might solve this problem by simply ordering a dumpster and throwing everything into it, but most of us are not so environmentally unscrupulous. A better option, for those with a conscience, is to put together a share list—of individuals, charities, resale shops, and other organizations that might be interested in your excess stuff.

Start by making a list of family members and friends who might want some Things. Note down the kinds of objects each seems to like, for example, Sam: books, music, stamps; Joan: clothes, dishes; Winston: toys, clothes.

Then call your community's waste management department. Ask them to send you any information they have on recycling as well as other disposal options. After that, hit the yellow pages. Call charities and ask them whether they pick up items, when they're open for drop-offs, what kinds of items they accept, and whether there's a limit on the quantity. Call resale shops and find out the same information, as well as what sort of commissions they take and how their financial transactions work. Go onto E-bay and find out how to register. Call groups that you think might have flea markets or collective yard sales and find out how they operate. Jot down numbers of hauling services for items you can't dispose of any other way.

Enter all the information into a database alphabetically by category, print it out, and keep it where you can find it. If you're afraid you'll lose it, tack it to the wall over the phone. Be prepared to distribute your list to family and friends who might use the same information. Or enlist the help of others from the beginning and make it a group project. Learning how to dispense with your unwanted Things is a crucial step in moving them out of your space and your life—a step you'll rely on again and again.

55. IT'S JUST A PROBLEM.

Are you freaking out at the sight of a pile of unpaid bills? It's just a problem. Does your overflowing closet fill you with shame? It's just a problem. Are you furious at your spouse for leaving papers all over the dining room table *again*? It's just a problem.

Negative emotions become crippling when you allow yourself to define a situation not as a problem but as a catastrophe. The pile of bills becomes the first step toward losing everything you own; the overflowing closet is evidence of your weak character; the paper-spreading spouse is trying to make you crazy. If you crave the feeling of adrenaline surging through you, go on extrapolating and projecting up the kazoo—but don't expect to get rid of big clutter that way. While you're busy catastrophizing, you're unlikely to pay those bills, clean out that closet, or have a constructive discussion with your spouse. Meanwhile, the clutter piles just get bigger.

If, on the other hand, you're willing to quiet yourself and begin to act decisively, the words "It's just a problem" can work magic. These words act like an automatic sprinkler system in cooling down over-heated emotions. Once the fire is out, the wheels in your brain begin to turn again, considering this option and that, weighing consequences, and jumping outside the box to discover win-win solutions. And for keeping the peace between would-be enemies, a problem-solving approach has proven itself many times over. If your spouse leaves messes, saying, "Honey, we have a problem" is likely to get you a lot further than, "Why don't you ever pick up after yourself?"

Whether we're talking interpersonal or intrapersonal, "It's just a problem" is part of living clutter-free.

56. MAKE A CONTAINER
STASH.

Organizing is largely a matter of matching the right Things with the right containers. This task can be bewildering. When your possessions are jumbled together, it's hard to know exactly what containers you'll need to sort and store them. Have faith: your needs will become clearer as you begin to group like objects together. In the meantime, you can begin collecting all the empty containers you have in one place and also go pick up a few basic types of containers if you don't already have them.

Designate a specific area for your container stash. This can be an empty closet, a couple of shelves, or just the corner of one room. Then do a container scan: comb the whole house from attic to cellar, and every time you come across any sort of empty container, put it in this area. All kinds of containers qualify: cardboard boxes, plastic boxes, wooden boxes, baskets, jars, cans, paper bags, plastic baggies, garbage bags, accordion folders, hanging folders, file folders—anything that can hold something else. (In general, boxes are better for storage than bags are, because they're more durable, neater, and easier to stack.)

Certain basic containers you're almost sure to need. Bankers' boxes are wonderfully versatile, portable, and easy to store, either collapsed when unused or assembled when used. They usually come in packages of six, and you should always have a couple of packages on hand. See-through plastic boxes are another staple of organizing. The sizes you'll want to get will depend on the kinds of Things you own—you'll almost certainly want some shoe-box-sized and some shirt-box-sized ones, which fit nicely on closet shelves, but you may want some other sizes as well. I'm also fond of Rubbermaid "File Totes," boxes the size of a small file drawer in which hanging files can be hung. I use them not only for papers but also to store memorabilia, books, and other small items. Plastic dividers and small boxes are useful for drawers, although stationery or check boxes will also work. If you have a lot of photos (see #80), you'll want to get a bunch of special photo boxes, which are generally covered with decorative paper. Avoid oversized cardboard boxes and trunks, which may be too heavy to move when filled.

All these basic containers are widely available at office, home, and organizing specialty stores. While it's a good idea to stock up on these types, don't buy other, more specialized containers until you're sure you'll use them. The trouble is, it can be hard to remember when you're at home with your stuff what specialized containers are available. If there's an organizing store in your area, spend half an hour there familiarizing yourself with the stock and ask for a catalog. Store the catalog with your container stash and consult it again when you need it.

As you sort, purge, and organize the items in your home, house them in containers from your stash. Use the containers you have, even if they're not ideal. Then look through your catalog and put more appropriate items on a shopping list. Don't put off containing items for lack of the perfect container: anything uncontained is clutter, and it's better to use the wrong container than to leave Things in piles.

57. ON TASK OR OFF TASK?

Some people, when they have a job to do, have little difficulty progressing from A to B to C without ever getting off track. It doesn't occur to them to leave off and go do something else in the middle of the project. Others are forever getting sidetracked and consequently rarely finish anything. This is a matter of brain chemistry and personal work style, but continually going off track can be a prime source of clutter. When you leave off in the middle of an activity, you usually leave some Things behind. And if the activity itself is reducing clutter, the piles stay where they are.

Pick a day, any day at all. Throughout that day, every fifteen minutes, ask yourself the question, "Am I on task or off task?" and note down the answer. If you're off task, that is, not doing what you started out to do, get back on. Use a timer that you can keep resetting for another fifteen minutes each time it goes off.

When you spend a day, or part of a day, tracking in this way, you raise your awareness of on task versus off task a little more on other days. Sometimes you'll still choose to go off task—rigidly linear people miss out on a lot—but you'll know that's what you're doing. If you do choose to go off task, you'll do so consciously and be aware of any clutter consequences. Then, once you're back on task, you can take care of whatever clutter your sidetrip created.

58. USE BINDERS AND
PLASTIC SLEEVES.

Do you have an allergy to filing containers, even those with open tops? If so, perhaps you'd be willing to put your papers in three-ring binders? I've worked with people who have whole shelves filled with binders and no filing containers at all. There's nothing wrong with this if it works for you. Binders are convenient, portable ways to store papers. You don't have to dig through anything to get to a binder—you can just reach over and grab it off the shelf. And you can carry it around without anything falling out.

Binders are the organizing device of choice for standard $8\frac{1}{2}$-inch-by-11-inch papers that you need readily available for reference and want to keep in a particular order. I use binders for newsletters, which often come with holes already punched, and some of my clients use them for papers from mutual funds. Add plastic sleeves, and you can put papers of all sizes in a binder. These are great for recipes, instructions, and kids' art and schoolwork. You can also buy special sheets for photos and business cards. (I don't recommend the ones for business cards, as you can't keep the cards in alphabetical order without constantly moving every card in the book—use a Rolodex instead.) Teachers and public speakers also use plastic sleeves in a binder to keep overheads in order when giving a lecture.

Binders come in various widths and materials. Choose one that's the right size for its contents. The thickest ones tend to be awkward, so split a large pile of papers into several smaller ones. Attach a clearly marked label to the spine of each binder. To make binders easier to identify, use a different color for each one or, if you have a lot of them, color-code by subject.

Be sure to get a *good* hole punch for unpunched papers. (A poor-quality hole punch will cause you more frustration than is worth the money you'll save.) Your punch should be sturdy enough to cut through at least ten papers at a time and also be easy to clean out. Electric hole punches make punching quick and easy.

Storing binders on shelves can be awkward if most of them aren't completely filled and thus are shaped like a wedge. The outside binders tend to turn inward as you add more binders on a shelf. To counter this, put all the binders in upright magazine holders or a vertical sorter.

Knowing when to dismantle binders is as important as knowing when to use them. While you may use a binder when taking a class or attending a conference, when it's over you're usually better off taking the papers out and filing them categorically, recycling anything extraneous. You can drastically reduce the volume of papers and binders this way, and because binders are reusable, you'll have a system ready for *new* papers and projects.

59. KEEP THE PAPERS MOVING ON.

Whole books have been written on paper management, many of which have excellent ideas about filing. When it comes to everyday life, however, files are far less important than action systems, through which you keep incoming papers moving until they're either out the door, in a recycle bin, or in a "to file" box. When papers come in, whether by mail, printed out E-mail, door-to-door leafleting, or your children's smudgy hands, immediately sort them or deposit them in a "to-sort" basket (see #45).

When you're ready to sort, stand next to a recycle bin and toss everything useless into it. Don't bother to open envelopes if you're really sure they're junk mail. Then divide what's left into three piles: items to send or give to somebody else, action items, and file items. Get rid of the Send/Give pile ASAP by mailing or handing papers over to their proper recipients. Meanwhile, put the File items—papers you want to put away—in a to-file box. Its size depends on how often you're able to file and how many papers you typically have. Schedule filing time in your planner within the next week to empty the box.

This leaves the Action items. Pull out all unpaid bills and urgent papers. If you have only a few, set up containers for bills and urgent items and use a simple in box for the rest. If you have a lot of papers, label colored folders with specific actions, such as "write," "e-mail," "copy," or "phone," and set them in a tiered vertical sorter on top of your desk. Set a specific time to look inside the folders every day.

Remove bills from their envelopes, write the amounts and due dates in big letters on the outside of the envelope, and put the bills in their container in order of due date. Recycle all inserts and extraneous material to cut down on volume.

Now pay all outstanding bills and perform all urgent actions. When you've finished, toss waste papers in the recycle bin, put keepers in the to-file box, affix stamps to envelopes, and take them to the mailbox. Then, if you have time, start working on the papers in your in-tray or action system. Keep the papers moving on!

60. PUT UP A PEGBOARD.

Pegboards aren't the most beautiful or newfangled piece of organizing equipment, but they're a great tool for increasing visibility and keeping all sorts of odd-shaped Things easily accessible. A pegboard's standard use is for tools and/or laboratory equipment, but it may also be useful in kitchens, art studios, and other areas. Instead of hiding items away in a drawer or a tool box, all the equipment is right there where you can see it and easily reach it. Pegboards also make use of vertical space that might otherwise remain unused.

Measure the area you want to cover with pegboard, then go to your lumberyard and have it cut to your specifications. Also buy some pegboard hooks and brackets of various types, and some washers. Glue the washers to the back of the pegboard with superglue to provide the space needed behind the board for pegboard-hanging hardware. Then, once the pegboard is in place, hang Things to your heart's content.

You'll probably want to organize your pegboard by categories, with all the screwdrivers together, all the hammers, and so forth. Fasten containers to the board for nails, screws, and other small items. If you're really sure you know where you want your tools to go, you can trace an outline of a tool on contact paper and attach it to the pegboard. Or, if you'd rather, use labels to show where different items go. Decorate the pegboard as creatively as you like.

One warning about pegboards: because your tools are out there for everyone to see, they may have a tendency to disappear at the hands of housemates and others who share your space. To counter this, post a sign next to the pegboard with rules and regulations about what tools can be borrowed and when they need to be returned. Next to the sign, put up a sign-out sheet so you can know who's using what.

61. PUT THINGS BACK EVEN
WHEN YOU'RE RUSHED.

Overcommitted people who spend a lot of time racing from place to place are a prime source of business for professional organizers. Nevertheless, not all overcommitted people are plagued with big clutter. Many remain relatively clutter-free because no matter how busy they are, they still manage to put Things back, or at least to *ballpark* them, which means putting them near—though not exactly—where they belong.

The problem is, when you're in crisis mode, leaving Things out becomes automatic. The lower centers of the brain are simply trying to save you time any way they can. This is where you need to outsmart your brain.

The first step is to consciously notice—using the higher centers of your brain—what you're doing. Choose a day to self-monitor for automatic crisis cluttering. Keep asking yourself how hurried you feel. If you feel rushed, how are you responding? What objects are you leaving where? How long would it really take you to put them away? Would taking a few more seconds to ballpark them really make you late? What would happen if you *were* a few minutes late? Whom would you displease? Is it someone you can afford to annoy?

Now try putting Things away for one day no matter what and weigh the consequences at the end of the day. How did you function throughout the day? How do you feel now? Being able to put Things back quickly depends partly on knowing where each item belongs. Setting up definite homes for Things—one type of Thing, one home—may, in fact, enable you to save the time previously spent looking for possessions so that you have enough time to put them back. Once you start living that way, you'll love it. You'll save time, feel less stressed, and have everything at hand when you need it.

62. CLEAN-UP TIME!

You're a little kid in preschool kicking your legs under your chair, and your papier-mâché mask is as finished as it's going to be. You've just picked up a nice, gluey glob of paper to fling at the kid on the other side of the table when Ms. Betsy stands up and shouts, "Clean-up time!" Suddenly the room wriggles to life. You drop the glob and join the other kiddies, already busy poking brushes into coffee cans, balling up sticky newspapers, and hurling matchbox cars into plastic shoeboxes. Before long everything is back where it belongs and you're rolling out rugs for your nap. Wouldn't it be nice if there were still a Ms. Betsy in your home or workplace to shout, "Clean-up time!" every time you finished building a shelf or typing a report? Some of us may still need this kind of incentive.

Pick a day and resolve that you'll make clean-up time a part of every activity for the entire day, no matter how rushed you are. If you have trouble remembering, put up little clean-up time notes in the areas where you work or play. Each time you clean up, ask yourself how you feel. Anxious? Rebellious? Soothed?

If you feel rebellious, against whom are you rebelling? Is it someone in the present—a critical spouse, for example—or someone in your past? In either case, remember that as long as your actions are a reaction to someone else—whether you're trying to please or to annoy him or her—you're not your own person. Decide how much order you truly want in your life and use clean-up times to create it.

If you find it too constricting to have a clean-up time after each activity, you may want to schedule a single major session once a day and leave your stuff out the rest of the time. If you choose to go this route, it's important to stick to your scheduled time, no matter what. Write it in your planner in big block letters every day for a week so you won't forget: CLEAN-UP TIME. And don't forget that after clean-up time comes nap time. Get ready to roll out your rug.

63. PLAN A DINNER PARTY THREE MONTHS FROM NOW.

How long has it been since you had someone over for dinner? Have you been putting it off until your house is perfectly organized? Don't. Instead, set a date for three months from now.

Yes, I said *three* months, and you should start issuing invitations after two. What's that? Preposterous, you say? You couldn't possibly—there's too much to do, your place is a mess, you don't have the right dining room set, your dishes don't match, the dog's teeth need cleaning, and there's that big ugly stain on the carpet.

Do it. If you're like most of us, knowing that people are coming over for a big event will get you de-cluttering like nothing else. Once you've got that date on the calendar and you know that people are actually going to show up and *see* your place, you'll discover you can do far more than you ever thought. Let the vision of happy, candlelit faces around a splendid table entice you into outdoing yourself.

Besides, you don't have to de-clutter your whole house to have people over, just the parts they're likely to see. This means the living room, dining room, kitchen, hallways, and at least one bathroom plus, if it's your responsibility, the outside of the building. Close doors to all the rest of the rooms if you need to. You may think you can't make even this much of your home respectable that fast, but I'll bet you can. The trick is to refrain from messing with papers and other small items you encounter along the way. Anything you don't have time to sort you can put into boxes, which you'll store in the rooms to be closed off. Once you've cleared out excess items, give all the public rooms a good cleaning, or hire a cleaning service to do so. Put pictures on the walls, knickknacks in appropriate places, a tablecloth and candles on the table, and you're ready to go.

Remember, your party area doesn't have to be perfect. Be selective about whom you invite. Don't ask your Aunt Jessica if you think she'll sneak around looking in cupboards and drawers, but do ask people whose company you truly enjoy. If this includes an intimate friend or two whose support you can enlist, so much the better. Do everything you can to make your space nice for your guests, but once they've arrived, relax and have fun. The point of having a party is not only to motivate you to get started with de-cluttering but also to reverse the pattern of putting off living until you're perfectly organized. If this is what you've been doing, you're due for a change.

64. STORE IT WHERE YOU USE IT.

Imagine a house in which kitchen utensils are kept in an upstairs bedroom, bed sheets in the kitchen cupboards, toiletries in the attic, motor oil in the bathroom, and clothes in the garage. Such a household might provide its occupants with plenty of aerobic exercise, but it would also consume an enormous amount of time and energy.

Storing items near where you use them is a cardinal principle of spatial organization. The assumption is that you'll want to devote as little time and energy as possible to getting Things out and putting them back. That's the theory, but it doesn't always turn out quite that way.

When people don't store Things where they use them, sometimes it's because they haven't given any thought to where they do what. To clear away the fog, make a list of the activities in which you engage—or would like to engage—in each room. Then ask yourself if you now have the items you need for each activity in the designated room. Within each room, you may want to set up activity areas for specific endeavors—a TV area, a reading area, a music area, and so forth.

In some cases, it might not be practical to store items in the room where you use them. For one thing, you might use the same items for different activities, using scissors for sewing, wrapping packages, and cutting your hair, for example. Does this mean you have to have three pairs in three different areas? It depends on whether you'd rather spend the money for more scissors or do extra legwork and probably leave scissors out more often.

Also, certain kinds of containers are designed to hold certain kinds of items, and the containers you need might not fit the room where you need them. You might do most of your reading on the living room couch, for example, but have no wall space in the living room for bookshelves.

In short, storing Things where you use them, although important, is only *one* principle of organizing and must be balanced against other considerations such as simplicity (one type of Thing, one home) and spatial efficiency (making the best use of available containers to contain as many items as appropriately as possible). Conflicts between principles always pose dilemmas. Is it better to keep your books downstairs next to your reading chair, where there's no room for bookshelves, or upstairs on the shelf? Is it better to keep different kinds of glue in different rooms or have them all in one central glue place so your mind won't have to remember so many different homes? How you resolve such dilemmas will depend on your own particular strengths and needs.

65. WHAT DO I *REALLY* NEED?

Do you crave abundance? Do you have trouble letting go of excess Things? If so, consider doing a personal needs assessment using psychologist Abraham Maslow's famous "Hierarchy of Needs."

According to Maslow, there are five basic categories of human needs, which people tend to gratify in ascending order if they have the freedom to do so:

1. Physiological—food, water, shelter, sex, warmth, medicine

2. Safety—order, predictability, balanced bank accounts, locks on doors

3. Love—hugs, listening, connecting, belonging

4. Esteem—power, achievement, competence, prestige

5. Self-actualization—being all you can be, doing what you were meant to do, learning, discovering, exploring, experimenting

Write down each need and consider how well you are meeting it. Which of your five needs is the strongest? What needs are you trying to meet with superabundant material Things? Are these basic needs that the objects are supposed to meet, or are they needs higher up in Maslow's hierarchy? Note that only physiological and some safety needs can be met by tangible objects—the rest are for intangibles. Are you trying to meet intangible needs with symbolic, tangible substitutes—buying expensive clothes instead of working to improve your body image, for example?

Once you begin asking yourself what you *really* need and look for a way to get it, you'll find it easier to letting go of excess Things.

66. DO IT THE EASY WAY.

Many of my organizing clients seem to confuse organization with complexity. They hire me, expecting that I'll devise some elaborate system that will solve all their problems, and they are often surprised by the simplicity of my recommendations. They seem to believe that if we can do something complicated enough, all their clutter will disappear. This is the very opposite of the truth; where organizing is concerned, easiest is nearly always best.

Two particular areas in which I often see people trying to get too complicated are paper management and time management. I find myself recommending simpler and simpler paper-management solutions the longer I continue to help clients with organizing. Most of the systems recommended in books are far too complicated for individuals struggling with paper piles.

For example, when I first started out, I sometimes recommended the "tickler file" system for action papers. This involves having folders for each day of the month and for each month of the year that you keep moving back. It's a fine system for those who came out of the womb organized, but it made most of my clients feel overwhelmed and confused, so I stopped suggesting it.

Even dividing action items into folders by action—to phone, or to write—may be too much if your mind doesn't categorize easily. Believe it or not, for many people a plain in-box is the action system of choice, especially if they don't have a lot of papers. (If you opt for this method, try to keep the papers that need to be dealt with first at the top. Shuffle through them every day to remember what's in the box and you'll be fine.)

The quest for complexity can be crippling, not only in managing papers but also in managing time. In working with new clients, I've often been astounded by the number of planners and other time-management devices people were trying simultaneously to use. One woman had six different planners for six different areas of her life, all filled with long, complicated lists. I advised her to get rid of all but one and combine all her to-dos in a single planner.

Standard planners typically offer all sorts of extra pages for different functions, which may make people feel overwhelmed. Likewise with electronic planning devices, which may have more functions than are comfortable for a beginning user. I advise people not to try to use everything new at once, but to start with a simple schedule and a to-do list. Time-management systems can bring out the rebellious side in many of us, and we're less likely to self-sabotage if we make changes slowly.

When your thoughts start to branch and rebranch, making simple tasks far more complicated than they need to be, you may experience an out-of-control feeling. I call this *complectifying,* a form of compulsivity. Most people's minds compulsively spin out ideas sometimes, and artists may sometimes relinquish control and allow this to happen on purpose. Notice when this starts to happen and say to yourself, "This is just my brain complectifying." Then mentally back up and shift down to a more basic level by asking yourself, "What's most important to me? What is it I'm really trying to do here?"

Simplicity is a key principle of organization. Whatever you're doing, if you do it the easy way it will be more likely to work. Strangely enough, this isn't always our first instinct, but once you learn to do it, you'll find it makes all the difference.

67. KEEP THE BOOKS
MOVING ON.

Books flow through the world like water. All over the planet books collect into puddles, lakes, even oceans (also known as libraries and bookstores) where people go to imbibe their precious contents. Books continually flow from one pair of hands to another, from one building to another, from one generation to another. The physical books are tangible vehicles through which intangible stories and ideas circulate, and this circulation is as vital to the future of humanity as water.

I have the good fortune to live in a town that facilitates the flow of books to the maximum. The local public library holds frequent book sales where people donate used books and others buy them for next to nothing. The town is also filled with bookstores—new, used, and rare—and the University of Michigan library system is not only one of the largest in the world but it can also acquire virtually any book in existence through interlibrary loan. Nevertheless, my clients here often seem to believe that if they sell or give a book away, they'll never have access to a copy again. (I can hardly blame them, as I have far more books myself than I'll probably ever read.) Ann Arbor is a town populated by biblioholics.

We book-lovers can find letting go of books exceptionally difficult. There's no place we'd rather be than seated in a well-lighted easy chair in a study lined with bookshelves. Books open whole worlds to us; how can we not love them? But for the bookish, this love might also be about security: books protect our mental health from more reality than we can handle (though they may also sometimes suggest ways to cope). The worse off the state of the real world, the more we crave the imaginary world of books. I've survived many a turbulent airplane flight untraumatized with the help of a good mystery. Shy people carry books around to hide their noses in rather than converse with strangers. Professionals may feel that they're competent in their chosen field only if they own every major book ever published in it, even in fields where knowledge becomes rapidly outdated.

If you're bookish yourself, I'm not suggesting that you ignore the needs that books meet in your life and stop collecting them at all. But when books begin to fill up bathroom shelves, kitchen cupboards, and linen closets and are stacked all over the fireplace hearth, even though you have a reasonable number of bookshelves in your home, it's probably time to become more selective.

Keep a share box for books near where you typically read (see #54). Whenever you finish a book, ask yourself if you're likely to ever look at it again. If the answer is no, put it in the box. I rarely keep novels unless they're classics, and I'm even selective about which classics I keep. The same goes for self-help books and other light nonfiction. (If you want to put *this* book in the box once you've absorbed its contents, you have my permission. Better to give it away than have it turn into unused clutter.)

At least once a year, do a cold-book scan. A cold book might be hot to others, but it no longer turns you on. Start at the top of your house and work your way down to the basement, looking at every book in the house. Consider your information needs—does this book meet any of them? How up-to-date is the information—and is the Internet an equally good source for it? If it's a book you've been planning to read, how long has it been waiting? Have your interests changed since you bought it? A rule some people follow with books is the one-in, one-out rule: every time you bring a new book into the house, another has to go into the share box.

Scanning for cold books is a lot easier if your books are separated by category and in alphabetical order. With each new scan, try to look at the books with new eyes. Along with thinning out your collection, you'll rediscover gems you'd forgotten and you'll be more familiar with the whereabouts of your books for the next time you're looking for one.

Once you've filled up some share boxes, take them to a library or resale shop. Caution: lifting boxes of books can be hard on your back. For safety, do not use boxes longer than seventeen inches and use only those with handles for carrying. If you think carrying a book-filled box might injure you, ask someone for help.

68. MAKE A HOME FOR
OFFICE SUPPLIES.

As you de-clutter and re-de-clutter on your way to clutter freedom, you may come across a yellow legal tablet here, a package of
dividers there, all jumbled together with other kinds of Things. Ironically, some office supplies such as folders, labels, and medium-point
pens are essential for organizing. To delete office supplies from the
clutter piles and thus shrink the piles forever after, you need to make
a special home for them.

Until you've cleared or acquired an appropriate permanent
home, start with just a cardboard box. Write "Office supplies" on the
outside with a felt-tipped marker and start throwing supplies into it
whenever you encounter them. Make a second box if the first fills up,
and perhaps even a third.

Meanwhile, consider what sort of home to create for your office
supplies. How big a home will depend on how many supplies you
typically have. If you have your own business, you'll probably need
more space than if you don't. In that case you may want to buy a
supply closet at an office supply store. Or you can use a wooden cupboard, or put extra shelves into a closet (closet organizing companies
can do this for you). If you have fewer supplies, a single shelf or a
few plastic drawers may be enough. Store small supplies in divided
trays or cardboard check boxes in your desk drawers or in plastic
minidrawers.

An added advantage of having a special home for office supplies
is that from now on you'll have a clearer idea of what's on hand so
you can restock items when they start to run low. And whenever you
need some graph paper or paper clips or pads of Post-It notes you'll
know exactly where they are—no longer in a jumble of clutter, but in
their very own homes.

69. USE BRIGHT COLORS.

Neurologically, we're designed to be more attracted to bright colors than dull ones and consequently to see them more easily. Colors appeal to our emotions as well as our thoughts, and emotional memory runs deeper and has more influence than cognitive memory. A sign with STOP printed in black and white would have far less impact than a sign painted red, a color that has a way of catching our attention.

We can use memory-assisting bright colors in diverse ways when organizing. Colors are especially helpful when you want to help children keep track of their stuff. Paint the drawers on your child's dresser different colors for different kinds of clothes. Store toys in containers with different-colored lids, or in colored plastic tubs on a wooden rack. Kids quickly begin to associate certain colors with certain homes for Things and may be more likely to put them away when color is involved.

Likewise with adults. Using color for paper management is a relatively recent development—amazingly recent, when you think about it. For some reason, it took the human race five millennia or so to realize that all hanging folders don't have to be yucky dark green, all pocket folders don't have to be pale reddish brown, and all file folders don't have to be boring cream-colored. Now, finally, at any office supply store you can buy folders of all three types—and many others—in a wide array of colors.

The question is how best to make use of this variety. Many organizers advise clients to "color code" their file folders. Although my own files are currently color coded into three categories—green for business, blue for personal, yellow for writing (I had to see if this changed my life—it didn't), I've come to think that color coding is probably less helpful for most folks than simply assigning colors to folders randomly. Color coding requires that you always have to have the right colors on hand and resist the temptation to use a different color if you run out of one of them. Using colors randomly, on the other hand, is less constricting and makes it easy to see a particular folder instantly, which may be a bigger plus than having everything matchy-matchy. If you use a system of action folders—to write, to phone, to copy—using a different-colored accordion folder for each action is essential to make the system work. Putting papers in different-colored binders (see #57)—with different-colored dividers—is another way of storing them more conveniently while exciting the senses.

Using folders and notebooks of different colors is not the only way to use color with papers. With plain manila folders or white boxes you can use different-colored labels, dots, Post-It flags, highlighters, markers, crayons, or pictures. The possibilities are almost infinite. And color doesn't just make papers easier to find, it also makes your world—and your life—a shade less dreary and a wee bit more fun.

70. LOOK UP.

If your space is none too roomy, lift thine eyes. You may have more space up there than you think, especially if you use it creatively. Do you see wall space where you could put brackets for shelves? Are there rafters where you could stow large items? Is the ceiling so high you could even build a loft? Are there hanging places for baskets or pots and pans? Is there room for hooks to get your bike off the floor and out of the way? What about adding an extra shelf above the one that's already in the closet? How about putting pictures on the ceiling?

It's only natural that most of us are slow to look up. If you've ever gone late to a movie and been forced to sit in the front row, you know why. Looking up for too long stiffens your neck and shoulders. With organizing, however, looking up can really pay off. In fact, part of the beauty of storing Things high up is that people *don't* look up most of the time. Thus, whatever's up there remains mostly hidden away, leaving more valuable floor space clutter-free.

71. KEEP THE MAGAZINES AND CATALOGS MOVING ON.

Do magazines and catalogs make up a significant proportion of your ongoing clutter? If so, that's good news. Magazine and catalog clutter is easy to reduce by taking a few simple steps:

- Cancel subscriptions to magazines you never read.

- Send postcards to businesses that send you catalogs you don't use, asking to be deleted from their list.

- Sort all the magazines and catalogs by type, then put them in order of date.

- Discard all expired catalogs and all catalogs for Things you never buy. This will not only get rid of catalog clutter but also make it harder for you to buy what you don't need.

- Decide how many issues of each magazine you and others in your household can expect to read in the next month and put them in your livingroom magazine holder. If you don't have such a holder, buy one. Purge this holder once a month.

- When going through magazines, tear out articles you want to read later and put them in an accordion folder next to your reading chair. Once you've read the article, if—and only if— you've found it uniquely useful, either put it into a binder with other uniquely useful articles or scan it into your computer and recycle the hard copy. If it's not uniquely useful, recycle it immediately. Before you spend a lot of time saving magazine articles, though, consider that any information voguish enough to appear in a magazine is probably also available on the Internet. And remember: public libraries typically have extensive, up-to-date magazine collections.

- Decide how much shelf space you want to devote to storing whole magazines and buy enough upright magazine holders to fill this space. Fill the holders close to capacity with the most recent issues and donate or recycle the rest. Whenever you add a new issue, discard an old one.

- Once every three months, do a magazine and catalog scan and move the magazines through the system.

Moving magazines along is easy and can reduce clutter dramatically. Follow these simple steps on a regular basis and enjoy another aspect of clutter-free living.

72. PUT A TRASH CONTAINER
IN EVERY ROOM.

You're sitting in your favorite chair, having just finished a bag of tortilla chips. Switching on the TV, you roll the bag into a ball and look around for a place to toss it. There isn't one. Getting up to deposit the bag in the kitchen wastebasket—the only trash container in your apartment—is too much trouble; instead you throw it on the floor, along with the scratch paper from the project you're working on, several dirty Kleenexes, and an old *TV Guide*.

If this sounds familiar to you, get up *right now* and find some kind of container—a brown paper bag or cardboard box will do—to position in each room of your home or workplace that doesn't already have a wastebasket. In a large chamber or office with several desks, you may want to use more than one container. Use whatever you have temporarily, but make a list of rooms that need permanent trash containers and buy them ASAP.

Plain plastic or wicker wastebaskets are fine for most rooms, but get a tall can with a lid for the kitchen garbage. Line the kitchen trash pail with a plastic bag. In my experience, the kind with a pedal is easier to use than the kind with a little swinging door. (For years I endured the aggravation of a plastic kitchen garbage pail with a swinging door that fell off every time I used it before I finally replaced it with a metal one with a pedal. This cost about $50 and gave me a new lease on life.) Don't forget waste containers for the basement rooms and the garage, and be sure you have an outside garbage can or two with a tight-fitting lid. If the lid is loose, put bricks on top to keep animal scavengers out. For easy transporting to the curbside, get a garbage can with wheels.

In rooms where you already have a trash container, you may still need to rethink its location. The balance to strike here is between appearance and convenience. Probably, you're not going to want to set a wastebasket in the middle of your livingroom floor. Place it somewhere discreet, but easily reachable. In the bathroom, most folks hide the wastebasket in a cupboard, though this makes it harder to get to than if it's out in the open.

At least once a week, go around and empty all the individual wastebaskets into a central one, pulling out anything that can be recycled and putting it in a recycle bin. When you're finished, carry the trash from the central wastebasket out to the garbage can and, if it's trash day, wheel the can out to the curb. Then wipe or rinse out the individual containers and return them to their homes.

73. MAKE A PET-CARE PLACE.

Pets these days require all sorts of paraphernalia: hairbrushes, combs, shampoo, flea repellent, medicines, deodorizers, eye droppers, ear droppers, tooth brushes, toothpaste, and many other items. If these are scattered all over the house, not only will you have more clutter but also you're less likely to make use of them routinely, depriving your furry darlings of the best possible care. That's why it's a good idea to set up a special place just for pet supplies.

Your pet-care place doesn't have to be anything fancy. A single shelf might be all you need. Use a few plastic shoeboxes or a set of plastic minidrawers to store smaller items. Store extra leashes, brushes, and small items in baggies to keep them separate. If possible, set a comfortable chair near the pet-care place where you can sit while performing your pet duties.

Now, consider your pet routine. What chores do you need to perform for each pet and when? Make a checklist of daily chores required to care for each pet and post it on the wall near your pet-care spot. If you aren't doing some of the chores regularly, write them in your planner or PDA until they become habits. Each day, after you've finished caring for your pets, pull the hair out of brushes and return all the supplies to their homes.

74. PURGE YOUR TOILETRIES.

I once worked with a client who was an Avon representative, helping her to organize her inventory. Her basement was filled with lotions and powders, perfumes and oils, not to mention the myriad noncosmetic products Avon makes. This woman educated me on the longevity of cosmetics. Most perfumed cosmetics, she said, begin to lose their scent after a year or so. Also, used lipsticks and compacts begin to attract bacteria over time and should be discarded if they're more than a year old.

I went home and began tossing ancient vials of sour cologne, empty deodorant bottles, and a whole slew of old lipsticks and compacts. This opened up a lot of space and made it easier to organize the rest of my newer, fresher cosmetics. I bought a little two-shelf rack for the toiletries we use most and set it on the counter, designated another small basket for my perfumes, and then organized everything else in the drawers under the counter.

Where toiletries are concerned, following the "one type of Thing, one home" rule can mean the difference between order and chaos. We now have a well-established hair drawer, face drawer, tooth drawer, shaving drawer, and soap drawer as well as a pouch for nail stuff and another for the cosmetics I use every day. This one-type-of-thing-one-home system makes it easy to put toiletries away after you've used them, and easier to find the next time. To keep small items such as hairpins from mingling in bathroom drawers, use plastic dividers or old check boxes. If your bathroom doesn't have drawers or a medicine cabinet with shelves, consider getting plastic drawers designed to fit in odd-shaped spaces. Wipe off dusty items with a damp sponge before you put them away.

Purging your toiletries and organizing your bathroom sink area is a relatively easy task and makes a nice pocket of order in your home—a great starting point for de-cluttering. When you've finished, take inventory and make a list of items that need to be replaced. Then wash your face and make yourself gorgeous, noticing how good it feels to have everything you need at your fingertips.

75. DON'T PILE,
CONTAINERIZE.

The trouble with piles is that they have a tendency to merge. When two piles accumulate side by side, as the piles continue to grow, the edges start to blur together until two piles become one pile—and two identities become one. The book pile plus the shoe pile becomes the book-shoe pile. Then the book-shoe pile merges with the paper-CD pile to make a book-shoe-paper-CD pile—mush.

Once objects are contained, even if they're not well organized within the containers, clutter is out of the way. If you need to get rid of clutter quickly, just put all the small items in containers with lids, sorted or unsorted, and presto: no more clutter. Getting rid of the unsightly piles may make it easier for you to stand being in a particular room so you can then open up one box at a time and deal with it. Are you afraid that if you put Things in a box with a lid you'll never look at them again? This will happen only if you choose not to look. Things don't move themselves (see #2).

While organizers generally recommend sorting Things into boxes rather than piles, in practice boxes won't work for every job. When de-cluttering a clothes closet, for example, you probably won't use boxes for clothes that are on hangers but instead lay them out in piles on the bed. Do this with full awareness that piles may merge, knowing that the piles will remain there for only a few minutes before you put clothes either back into the closet or into a garbage bag to bring to charity or otherwise give away. With smaller objects you'll want to use sorting boxes—Keep, Share, Elsewhere, Recycle—perhaps breaking the Share box into separate boxes for each destination.

Where papers are concerned, containers are a must. Start out with just two boxes—File and Act—plus a recycle bin. Once you've sorted papers into these three containers, begin setting up folders for the File and Act systems (see #59).

For some of us, emotional roadblocks might make containerizing difficult. Examine what it feels like for you to put Things in containers. Does it make you a little uneasy? Are you more comfortable with free-flowing piles than having your Things walled up in boxes and drawers?

Now consider your relationships. Do you have trouble setting boundaries with others? Is it hard for you to say anything but yes? I've never done a study of this, but I'd be willing to bet that people who habitually let people spill over into inappropriate areas of their lives also let Things spill over the sides of containers and into piles. (If a psychology student out there is looking for a subject for a dissertation, be my guest!)

If containerizing doesn't feel comfortable, try breaking into it gradually. Start by putting just a few types of Things in containers and leave others floating around for the time being. One by one, containerize an additional type of item. Over time, you'll get used to containerizing more and more. As this happens, you might find that your relationships begin to change too. By setting boundaries with Things, you might establish a pattern that will help you to set better boundaries with people as well.

76. CATCH PEOPLE BEING GOOD.

For some of us, reducing ongoing clutter is not only a matter of changing our own habits, but also of encouraging others to change theirs. This can be difficult. It's especially challenging when the candidates for behavior change are close to you. In dealing with intimates, we can become frustrated and respond to our frustration by nagging and lecturing, strategies unlikely to get us what we want. What works better is to catch people being good.

Watch for a minor episode when a loved one makes any move at all, no matter how minute, to help turn chaos into order. It won't necessarily be the move you're determined the other person should make, but acknowledge it anyway. If, for example, it drives you crazy when your seven-year-old daughter throws her coat over a chair every afternoon when she comes home from school, she isn't necessarily going to suddenly hang the coat up without being reminded. But she might absentmindedly put a book back on the shelf after she's finished reading it. If she does, notice it and give her a love pat with a "good job!" Then, later, when she forgets to leave her dirty dishes on the dining room table after dinner and instead carries them into the kitchen, congratulate her again.

If the person you're dealing with is an adult, you might want to express your pleasure a little differently, but the same principle holds true. With adults you can be a little more long term, waiting until you've caught the person being good several times before saying anything. When you do, just thank the person and ask him or her what you can do in return: "Thanks for clearing off the table, honey—is there anything I can do for you?" In doing so, you affirm that this is a partnership in which you're willing to give as much as you take.

With one group of intimates, this approach can be tricky: adolescents. If you praise an adolescent too much for being helpful, he or she might become fearful of remaining a child-slave forever and deliberately *not* do what you want the next time. Thus, it's best to appeal to the young person's desire to be an independent adult: "Since you picked up after yourself, you can have the car tonight if you like," for example. Be sure not to sound triumphant, just matter-of-fact.

If you're dealing with someone to whom messiness comes more naturally than neatness, don't despair if the opportunities to reinforce positive behavior occur infrequently at first. Just watch for the one time that is the exception, even if it seems to happen by accident. If you acknowledge it with praise each time, you'll find that gradually, more and more often, the person will opt for order over chaos.

77. SQUARE THE CORNERS.

Okay, so you really can't seem to containerize your piles of papers, books, CDs, or magazines (see #75). Then, for heaven's sake, at least square the corners. If you've decided that containers aren't for you, it's possible to do without them and still have minimal clutter if you're willing to make the effort to keep corners squared so that piles stay neat and distinct.

Squaring corners simplifies the way the pile looks. When the corners aren't squared, items stick out, making a ragged edge. Take a few seconds to eliminate this edge on each pile, and the room looks 100 percent neater. In addition, piles won't merge into each other as easily when the corners are squared.

Why, then, do people *not* bother to square the corners on piles? The main reason is probably accommodation. When you've lived with ragged edges and sloppy piles long enough, you stop seeing them the way someone else would who just walked into the room. People who are more auditory than visual or kinesthetic learners may be less sensitive to the lining up of edges. Another possibility is rebellion. Some of us, early on, began to equate messiness with independence, defying Mom, Dad, or a third-grade teacher with our mess. (It's time to change that pattern.) And, of course, there's the simple lack of time and energy that most of us face.

Take a minute to look around the room you're in. What piles do you see? Are the corners squared? Now get up and go square the corners. When you're finished, look at the aligned piles. How do you feel? Soothed? Depressed? Like messing up the piles again? Whatever you feel, don't unsquare the piles. Just let any negative feelings flow through you until they abate.

Then go into the next room and square some more corners.

78. SCHEDULE A REGULAR
READING TIME.

Do you always seem to have more books, magazines, newspapers, newsletters, and other reading materials around than fit neatly into the space you have for them? Perhaps it's because you don't spend enough time reading, or read only one book at a time and never look at space-consuming periodicals. If that's the case, either cancel all your subscriptions or schedule a regular reading time in your planner or PDA.

Before your scheduled reading time, collect small pieces you want to read into an accordion folder—tear out articles from magazines and throw the rest away (see #71)—and books and magazines into a to-read box. Gather a few highlighters, pens, and a package of Post-It markers. Then settle back in your favorite chair.

Start with the contents of your article folder. Decide which ones you're going to read all the way through and which you're going to skim. Some articles you might be content to read and recycle; others you'll want to put into your to-file box when you've finished. Marking them with a highlighter and making notes in the margin will enable you to find the crucial materials more easily in case you want to refer to them again.

When you've finished reading individual articles, move on to whole magazines. Set a time limit for each magazine and read only what you can within that limit. Relax and enjoy flipping through pages, skimming here, reading there, until the time is up. Then tear out any articles you absolutely *have* to read later and put them into your article folder for your next session. Toss the magazine in the recycle bin.

Now spend some time on a good book. If it's fiction, you'll probably want to read it all the way through, but if it's nonfiction, be selective about what to read and what to skim. Ask yourself what you want to take away from the book in your hands, and if you own the book and it's not filled with gorgeous art, give yourself permission to mark it up if you need to. This will help you get more good stuff into your head so you can let the physical book go.

The biggest challenge will be dealing with all the interruptions that materialize once you're sitting in your reading chair. Let the phone ring (see #26), put up a "do not disturb" sign, or wear a special hat that signals to your family that you're to be left alone. Read behind a closed door, unless you're one of those people who concentrates better in Grand Central Station. If none of these strategies work, consider going somewhere else to read—to the library, a cafe, a nice park, or the lobby of a hotel. The result will be a smaller pile of reading clutter—and the pleasure of actually reading all that material you've been meaning to get to.

79. PURGE AND ORGANIZE
YOUR PHARMACEUTICALS.

Most medications don't last forever. Both prescription and over-the-counter drugs have expiration dates on them and should be thrown away after those dates. Having expired medications around can endanger your health, and they also contribute to clutter. Do yourself a favor and get rid of them.

If you're like most people, you have some medications in the kitchen and some in the bathroom, so be sure to purge both areas. Once you've cleared out all the expired products plus any you don't take anymore, organize what's left.

If you take any pills daily, I strongly recommend a pillbox with compartments for each day. These come in different sizes and can save your life. If your medication regimen is complicated, you might also want to make a chart to help you keep track of which medications you've taken each time. You might think you have a perfect memory, but you don't want to risk your health by learning that you don't.

As for the rest of your medications, store them in a kitchen cupboard or bathroom medicine cabinet. If you have children, make sure the location is inaccessible to them. If your child is a climber and ingenious, put a lock on the door.

Organize your medicine bottles so they make sense to you. Separate prescription drugs from over-the-counter medications and organize them by person. Use highlighters to color-code the labels to make mistakes less likely. Nonprescription medications are best organized by ailment: cold remedies, digestive medicines, pills for muscle pain, and so forth. Some medications might require refrigeration. Within categories, alphabetizing makes bottles easier to find. Wipe the outsides of bottles clean with a damp sponge.

Once your medications are organized, take inventory and consider if there's anything you need that you don't already have. While you're out, pick up a first aid kit and a good book on dealing with medical emergencies. Keep the first aid kit and book in your kitchen, where accidents are most likely to occur.

80. RETHINK YOUR PHOTO HABITS.

People take photos for many different reasons. Some take them to create a work of art. Some take them to serve as connectors with other people or with their own past. Some take them because they're afraid of forgetting. Some take them compulsively to keep from living.

If practicing the art of photography makes you happy, click away, but if you want to cut down on photo clutter, you might want to rethink your photographic habits. Is photography an art for you or a compulsion? Do you take pictures on trips and at family gatherings just because that's what your parents did? Is there more "should" involved than genuine pleasure? Do you take multiple pictures of views without people in them? If you're not taking the panoramics for art's sake, are you taking them because you think that's what you're supposed to do in response to a view? What would it feel like to buy a picture postcard and leave yourself free to look?

Also, whether you're on vacation or at home, do you feel obligated to photograph someone else's every waking moment? Is this out of genuine pleasure, or obligation? And how many photos of this person do you or they actually need?

What about collecting photos? Have you kept every single photo you and anyone else ever took, including pictures of people's thumbs and those so blurry you can't identify the subject? Are you haunted by guilt at not having put all of your photos into albums? If so, it's time to get real about the photos you already have.

First, get all of your unsorted photos together in one place. Buy three or four albums with plastic sheets that protect photos from yellowing and a bunch of special photo boxes with different patterns of paper on the outside, sold at organizing and office superstores. Enlist the help of others in your family and begin sorting. Discard pictures of poor quality or that bring back bitter memories. Discard duplicates (many photo shops offer a second set free, whether you need it or not), as well as near-duplicates. Decide on categories for each photo box. Sorting by event or time block works better than sorting by the people in the photos, as many photos will contain more than one person. Consider making boxes of photos to give to other family members. Label dividers with subdivisions within each category.

After you've sorted all the photos into boxes, go through them and choose a few of the best to put in your albums. Rather than make photo albums, you might want to make scrapbooks that include other memorabilia, though these will incorporate fewer pictures. Some organizers specialize in helping people to do this, and special stores sell scrapbook materials.

Owning a digital camera changes everything. This gives you the option of storing pictures on your hard disk and not printing them out at all, or printing out only your favorites. It makes sharing them over a long distance incredibly easy via e-mail or on virtual photo albums (www.ofoto.com, www.printroom.com). This can be another good way of cutting down on photo clutter. And if you want prints of particular pictures, you can print them out on a color printer using special paper, have prints made at a photo finishing store, or order prints over the Web.

Remember, your photos should bring you pleasure, not cause you guilt, obligation, regret, expense, and clutter. The choice, as always, is yours.

81. SET NUMERICAL LIMITS.

I sometimes ask my clients how many pairs of shoes or other particular items they think most people have. To me, the numbers they come up with often seem inordinately high. One woman, for example, couldn't imagine how anyone could survive with less than thirty sweaters. When I told her I usually kept about ten in my closet, she looked at me like I was crazy.

People who hang on to too much stuff frequently have an inflated idea of typical quantities, given the amount of space they have available. Obviously, a typical quantity is not the same for those who live in a small apartment as it is for those who live in a very large house. Yet even the owners of a mansion probably don't want to devote large amounts of space to storing a particular type of Thing. There is a point when even if you're fabulously wealthy it begins to seem decadent and excessive to have too many of something. Mrs. Marcos, with her shoes, is a case in point.

To eliminate excess then, it helps to set quantitative limits for yourself. But how do you know how much is enough and how much is too much? One way is to do a survey of people you know with relatively uncluttered households, asking them how many objects of different types they own. Try it with just one or two items and see how they respond. Your needs and interests may be different from those of your friends, but you might get a good reality check.

Ultimately, the best method is to determine what *you* actually need, along with a few frills to make life more pleasant. Take clothes, for example (see #49). What kinds of garments do you typically wear every day? Do you work from home, where you can wear sweatsuits all day, or do you dress professionally? Most people don't need more than two weeks' worth of clothing in any given season. How often do you wear dress clothes and of what type? What about exercise clothes? On this basis, set a number for each type of garment. Make a list of your clothing items:

10 sweaters

10 shirts

6 pair pants

5 turtlenecks

3 pair shorts

7 T-shirts

and so forth. Then get all your sweaters together, rank them in order of preference, and put anything below the top ten in a share box or bag (see #54).

Another method is to limit your Things by volume. Before doing so, make sure you have sufficient containers for each type of item. Then, simply let the volume of the container determine how many you'll keep. Be sure not to fill the closet, drawer, or shelf to the limit but instead to save space for new items that might come into your life. (Many people already use this strategy with books, papers, and magazines.)

Setting definite quantitative limits, whether by number or by volume, and staying within them can take a load off your mind. Freed from overwhelming excess, you can enjoy those items you've chosen to keep.

82. SAY WHAT YOU WANT—THE VERY BEST WAY.

Is someone in your household making major contributions to the amount of clutter around you? Would you like the person to stop? Tell him or her, in the very best way.

You could never tell him, you say. It wouldn't change anything. You've told her before and it didn't help. You can't teach an old dog new tricks. People are what they are. His parents were that way. She has A.D.D. He should know what you want without being asked.

Balderdash! A lot of clutter can be eliminated by opening your mouth and simply saying what needs to be said to the right person in the right way. If you don't say what you want, it's a cinch you're probably not going to get it. Most adults aren't mind readers, and most also want others' wishes voiced before they consider honoring them. If you've voiced your concerns to the person before, it might not have worked because you didn't articulate them in the very best way. To give yourself the optimum chance of success, here are some suggestions:

- Choose the right time: don't raise sticky issues when the person is tired, hungry, sick, or preoccupied.

- Empathize: consider the impact your request may have on the other person and let him or her know you're aware of the possible feelings involved.

- Be brief: don't lecture or berate—just say what you need to say.

- Be positive: instead of talking about removing a mess, talk about creating a beautiful, organized space.

- Ask for help: focus on what you're trying to achieve and how the other person might aid your efforts.

- Be respectful: let the person know that you respect his or her right to decide whether or not to do what you want.

- Maintain your autonomy: consider how you'll deal with it if the person refuses to do what you ask. Then do what you need to do.

- Use I-statements: start your request with "I need you to . . ." or "I want you to . . ."

- Ask permission to issue reminders: this protects you from charges of nagging.

- Limit your request: make it clear that you're not asking the person to change his or her whole personality, just a small aspect of behavior.

- Don't ask for everything all at once: consider which small behavioral changes would make the biggest difference to you.

- Be sure you have the person's attention: make eye contact and touch the person lightly if you have trouble connecting.

- Make sure the person really heard you: don't assume from an "uh-huh" that he or she did so and is willing to comply.

- Listen: give the person an opportunity to explain why he or she is unable to do what you ask.

- Be fair: express a willingness to do something the other person wants you to do in return.

Keep in mind that even if you follow all these suggestions, asking for what you want does not necessarily ensure that you'll get it. The other person might say no outright or, "Yeah, sure," and then fail to follow through. In that case, you'll have to take one of three possible courses of action: clean up the clutter yourself; hire someone else to clean it up; or leave the clutter where it is and try to get used to it. Which course you choose will depend on what's most important to you. If you're going to stay with the clutterer, remind yourself of the positives that outweigh the annoyance of dealing with his or her messes and let it go.

Whatever the outcome, saying what you want in the very best way is more productive than smouldering in silence. Once you've said your piece and found out what's what, you'll have a clearer idea of what to do next.

83. SET A TIMER.

We live in an age in which all sorts of electronic gadgets are available to help us manage time. Making use of them can help you create a more clutter-free lifestyle. The simplest timing device is a clock or watch that only tells you the time. Even this can be useful. Just noting down the time when you start and finish a task will give you a better sense of how fast you work and enable you to establish reasonable goals. Depressed people often overestimate how long a task will take and are surprised to discover that making their bed or doing dishes takes only a few minutes. Others underestimate how long jobs will take and are consequently always setting themselves up for failure by making long to-do lists that no one could possibly complete in the time allotted. Once you know how much you can do in a given span of time, planning becomes a lot simpler. Using a stopwatch makes this even easier. You don't have to write down the starting and ending times—the device does the math for you.

Most clocks and many watches are equipped with an alarm that you can set. This can help you to get up in time to de-clutter before you leave for work, or remember to take the trash out before the truck arrives. Alarms work by intruding on your senses, and the right alarm for you does whatever it needs to do to catch your attention. Some people don't hear a regular alarm clock ring but will respond if the sound is extra loud or goes on extra long. Others need a tactile sensation, a flashing light, or even the sound of a human voice. Alarms are available that feature all of the above. Some devices have only one alarm that has to be reset to go off again, while others have multiple alarms. These can help you to structure your day if you're following a schedule. Alarms may also be combined with written or spoken reminders.

A timer goes off not at a specific time, but after a particular length of time has elapsed. Some models, such as cube timers, can be set to go off at regular intervals—every ten minutes, for example. Timers can be a godsend to the distractible. If you're dawdling along on a de-cluttering task, set a timer and play Beat the Clock. To keep from getting sidetracked, set a timer to go off every fifteen minutes or so and every time it does, ask yourself if you're on task or off task. A timer can also help you get back to work after a break. If you're tired, set a timer for five or ten minutes while you relax, and get back to work when it beeps or buzzes.

The tricky part is to find the right timing device for you. A host of different possibilities are offered on the following Web sites: www.dynamic-living.com; www.independentliving.org; www.casio.com; www.datexx.com (offers cube timer); www.shoplifestyle.com. Before shopping for a new time gadget, you need to be clear about the problem you hope it will solve. Make sure that it's a problem for which a timing device is the solution. (So far, no device has been invented that can force you to get out of a chair, for example, though some can make it pretty unpleasant if you don't.)

If you do start using a timing device, don't use it all the time. Clock time doesn't come naturally to everyone, and doing what's unnatural day after day is stressful. Forcing yourself to live by the clock twenty-four/seven is like forcing a horse to wear a bridle all the time. Just as a good horseperson will take the bridle off and turn the horse out to pasture now and then, you need to go off camping once in a while and leave your watch at home.

84. IT'S JUST A GLITCH.

It's been a long time coming, but human beings are finally beginning to understand that everybody's brain is wired differently. Each brain has its own peculiar strengths and, no matter how brilliant, its own specific glitches—operations that don't work so well. I have various glitches and quirks myself of which I'm aware: a lousy sense of direction, internal distractibility, coordination problems, forgetfulness. Yet somehow I've managed to get by, compensating for some glitches and getting extra help in dealing with others.

What strengths and glitches different people have is mostly the result of subtle differences in neurochemistry and other biological phenomena. The wrong combination of glitches can make a particular type of work difficult. Some glitch combinations make it hard to do math, learn languages, or play baseball. And some make it hard to get organized.

Trouble is, people haven't always seen it that way. Most chronically disorganized people have heads filled with nasty tapes put there by the unenlightened, who were frustrated by their own messiness and didn't understand its complex causes. These people may have glitches themselves that affect patience or empathy. Unfortunately, the unenlightened still dominate many scenarios. When they voice their opinions—either in the world or in your head—they can gum up the works and make organizing operations even harder for your brain to perform. Hence the need for the words, "It's just a glitch."

"Why can't you get organized? What's wrong with you?" the person screeches.

"It's just a glitch," you answer quietly.

"How can you stand this mess? You are such a lazy slob."

"It's just a glitch."

"You should be able to clean this place up. You're just making excuses. You're trying to drive me crazy. I can't believe how selfish you are. It's all your fault. You're guilty, guilty, guilty."

"It's just a glitch."

Quietly repeat these four little words until the person has vented his or her frustration—which is genuine and requires empathy from you—and begins to burn out. Then, if you can, take advantage of the opportunity to explain that organizing, like math or languages, requires complex brain operations that are more difficult for some people than for others.

Repeating this phrase is worth doing even if the person is deceased, and accusing you only in your own mind. In that case, tell that person you didn't deserve his or her abuse, and repeat the words "It's just a glitch" in response to anything you imagine him or her saying in response. It won't change what the person said or did in the past, but you'll be able to problem-solve with a clearer head, tackling your own particular glitches to get rid of the clutter.

85. EVERYTHING HAS ITS PRICE.

At some point in the course of living more clutter-free it's bound to happen that you'll want or need something you got rid of when you de-cluttered. Chances are this will be something you can replace with a Thing you like even better than the original, but it's possible that it won't be. It's not impossible that you might end up longing for an irreplaceable letter, a valuable antique, or something else that you unthinkingly let go of and feel heartbroken over your mistake.

When this happens, the only thing you can do is remind yourself that everything has its price, including clutter-free living. Sure, you wish you still had the absent item, but consider what you've gained. Walk around your home and look at the clutter-free surfaces, the books lined up on the shelves, the clothes hanging neatly in your closet. Think about how your space used to look and how it made you feel. The Thing you no longer have, wherever it now may be, is just a Thing—a small price to pay for what you now have in its place: a home you can be proud of and a less stressful, more rewarding life.

Then turn on some music, make yourself a cup of tea, sit down in your favorite chair, and start enjoying all that you *do* have.

86. WHEN WILL I START AGAIN?

If you don't want clutter to perpetually reaccumulate, it's essential never to stop de-cluttering without having decided when you'll start again. This is critical whether you stop for five minutes to go to the bathroom or for five months to go on a trip. Many a de-cluttering effort has been derailed by a five-minute excursion that somehow extended into five years.

When the restart time will be depends on why you're stopping. If you have something more important than de-cluttering to do, plan to restart as soon as you're finished with whatever that is. If you're stopping because you're tired, consider how long it will take you to recharge, and in the meantime do whatever is necessary to refresh yourself—get a drink of water, have a snack, take a nap, or go on a short walk.

Along with deciding when to start again, you'll want to create a reminder. If the restart time is the same day, set a timer or an alarm (see #83). If it's on another day, schedule the next session into your planner or PDA. You can also ask others to remind you when the time comes.

To keep the continuity, be sure to leave reminders to show you where to start when you come back to your project. Label sorting boxes on the outside in big letters with a felt-tipped marker, put brightly colored Post-It notes on piles of folders, leave a note to yourself on the wall—"purged all the accounting files—start with the marketing folders," or "did sock drawer—do underwear next." Line boxes up and square corners wherever you can to leave the area looking as neat as possible before you walk away; the better the area looks when you leave off, the easier it will be to come back.

Commit to restarting, and keep your commitment. You'll be glad you did.

87. PRACTICE TOY-
POPULATION PLANNING.

Most children in developed countries have far more toys than they need. In families with young children, toys usually comprise a large proportion of household clutter. The solution is obvious: fewer toys.

Alas, decreasing the toy population can be challenging. There are many factors that keep families buried in toy clutter:

- Toys arrive as gifts from grandparents and other relatives and friends. It's one thing not to buy your child a toy he or she wants; it's another to take away a toy that someone else has already bestowed. Solution: talk with potential gift givers ahead of time and set limits; suggest that they give the child money to put in a savings account toward a larger item such as a bicycle, or tickets for an event he or she might enjoy.

- Children, like adults, are bombarded with messages from the media about what toys they should have. Solution: monitor the media messages your child absorbs and counter them with messages of your own that are more in keeping with your family's values.

- Children can be ridiculed for not owning objects that their peers have. Solution: empathize with your child's hurt feelings and teach your child how to respond assertively—not aggressively—to such behavior. Help your child to understand that the best things in life aren't Things.

- Parents may overidentify with their children and not want them to do without Things they remember wanting. Solution: recognize that this is about you and your own unmet needs, not what's necessarily best for your child. Rather than indulging yourself by giving your child everything he or she asks for, validate your child's feelings when you have to say no: "I guess you feel pretty sad that you can't have that truck you want, huh?" Learning to deal with feelings in response to a no is an important part of any child's education.

If your household is already overflowing with toy clutter, you need to take charge. If possible, coordinate toy-purging activities with purging of your own possessions, and explain to the child that we all have to get rid of excess Things from time to time. Help your son or daughter to imagine what a house would be like where no one ever got rid of anything.

Begin by collecting excess toys from common areas and putting them in each child's room or playroom. Gather together some plastic shoe boxes, cardboard boxes, and a garbage bag, and start sorting. Get rid of all irreparably broken toys and unidentifiable parts. Re-assemble sets, and sort larger toys into piles by type.

Box up any toys you're sure your child has outgrown and give them away (see #54). Then ask your child which of the remaining toys are his or her favorites. Keep these accessible and store the rest in well-labeled cardboard or plastic boxes in your storage area. If the child asks to play with a particular toy that's in storage, ask him or her to help you swap it for a toy that's easily available but underused.

Include your children in family Thing-disposal projects. If you have a yard sale, invite children to make money selling old toys; if you're filling a box for charity, ask the kids to put something in.

How you handle this issue may help determine whether your child grows up to struggle with clutter, debts, and other problems relating to material Things, or learns to deal effectively with the material world. Take the opportunity to have a positive effect—and then enjoy the results along with your child.

88. PUT INACTIVE FILES IN STORAGE.

One reason people don't file papers is that their filing cabinets are already bulging with inactive files that could just as well be put into storage, if not in the recycle bin. Inactive files are ones you don't currently need, though you might need them at some point in the future. Suppose, for example, that you used to teach college classes but you've stopped doing that for the time being. You're not sure you'll never teach again, but for right now your career has gone in a different direction. In that case, there's no need to keep all the old syllabi, lecture notes, and articles on teaching in your office taking up space you now need for the consulting business you've started.

Where tax papers are concerned, you need to keep relevant ones for seven years in case of audit—but the only situation in which you're likely to need them is if an audit actually takes place. The chance of this happening is small enough that it makes sense to store the papers away in your attic or basement rather than keeping them in space you can use for active files. If you should be audited, however, you'll be in deep trouble if you don't have the right papers: getting rid of them is not an option. Storage is the perfect solution.

If you're going to put files in storage, you need good storage containers. Replace from cardboard boxes with plastic file boxes, as they're less susceptible to mold, insects, rodents, and fire, and, if possible, put the boxes on shelves so you can get to them easily. Label each box on the outside in large, clear letters. Use hanging folders or manila envelopes inside the box so you can find the contents without a struggle. Purge outdated papers from storage every few years.

Putting papers in storage can involve a certain amount of strenuous effort. People who physically aren't up to the job may tend to put it off for that reason. If that's your situation, it's time to get real and hire or recruit help. This may be hard on your pride, but it's a lot better than winding up in bed with a strained back. It's also better than keeping deep storage papers in your filing cabinet and denying yourself the use of more convenient space for papers that you use in the here and now. Storage is the answer.

89. TAKE A WALK AROUND THE OUTSIDE OF YOUR HOUSE.

Do you live in a house? How long has it been since you've really looked at your home from the outside? What you see when you do is what your neighbors see all the time. If your porch and yard are filled with clutter, that's not just a problem for you—it's also an intrusion on others. Because you spend most of your time inside, you may not realize how depressing exterior messes can be, both to people's spirits and to property values.

To raise your awareness of outside clutter, make a point of taking a walk around your house once a month. Start at the front door, clipboard in hand (see #5) and take notes as you do your walk-around. Is there a saggy old couch or a rusty vacuum on your front porch? Such eyesores are commonplace in the student neighborhoods of any university town, but in standard residential neighborhoods they're out of place. Are there any screens or windows that need repairing? Is there a broken step? Are bicycles and toys scattered everywhere? Scan your lawn for bits of paper and weeds. Walk around to the side and scan the driveway and yard. Is one of your garbage cans lying on its side? Finally, the backyard: Is the sundeck covered with spilled birdseed? Is the firewood halfway across the yard? Make a list of everything that needs to be taken care of.

Then come inside and consider who can do each task and what it will cost. Don't put tasks off just because you can't do them yourself. Pick up the phone and make the necessary calls. Then get busy doing whatever you can yourself.

As you tackle each task, be sure to cross it off your checklist—and remember to walk around the house again, enjoying the fruits of your efforts!

90. DO A READY-TO-GO SCAN.

Why it is I don't know, but human beings have a way of collecting Things into boxes and bags, getting them ready to go out of their home or workplace, sometimes even putting them in the car, and then letting them sit. You fill a bag of clothes for the Salvation Army and leave it in your bedroom for six months. You fill a box with old dishes for the resale shop and it stays in your car. If you're doing something similar, ask yourself why. It may be because you're busy—or there may be more to it than that. All sorts of family dynamics, attachments, and fears can sometimes tie us up in knots. Something inside us resists finally handing it over, even though we know that afterwards we'll be glad it's gone.

At least once a month, take a walk around your home to see if there's anything ready and waiting to be removed from your space. Are boxes of books sitting in your hallway that should go to the library? Do you have stuff in your trunk that you could drop off? Don't be deterred by the expectation that you'll have another load to take to the same destination after you've done some more de-cluttering. Space is precious, and there's no law against making two trips to the same place. Maybe you needed to keep the bags sitting around for a while to wean yourself, but now it's time to let go and move it on.

91. PIGGYBACK YOUR HABITS.

Are you trying to establish a new clutter-reducing habit? The easiest way is to tie it to a habit that has long since become automatic. Suppose you're trying to establish the habit of making your bed every morning. You already get dressed by habit when you get up, so make a new rule: whenever you get dressed, you also make your bed. If making your bed is an old, established habit, you can piggyback another: whenever you make your bed, you also hang up your clothes. The formula is "whenever I ——, I also——." Easy. Think about what new habits you'd like to establish, sit down right now, and write out sentences using this formula.

A word of warning, however: the piggyback strategy will work only if you allow enough time in your schedule for the new task as well as the old. If you don't, you'll soon begin dropping the new task in order to save time. Making time to do a new job might mean making a decision *not* to do something else.

You also have to remember the new task. Until it becomes routine, you might want to put up a strategically located reminder sign. Tape it to the door going out of the bedroom, for example: Stop! Did you make the bed?

To reinforce the new connection, whenever you've finished the piggybacked task, verbalize the link: dressed, bed, dressed, bed, dressed, bed. Then, to reward yourself, step back and appreciate what you've done.

92. I DESERVE THE BEST.

Yes, I know you're not a millionaire who can afford gold dishes and diamond-studded dog leashes. That's not what I mean by "the best." What I mean is the best quality items that you already have or the best that you can currently afford.

In helping clients de-clutter, I'm often saddened by the poor quality of Things people force themselves to use even when they have other, much nicer ones. They might wear only ratty sweaters with holes in the elbows, for example, while brand-new cashmeres hang in their closet. If this is you, what's going on? Do you feel that you don't deserve quality? If so, let's get something straight right now: whoever you are, you deserve to wear the best you can buy.

If you grew up without nice Things, you might have gotten the idea that they were for other people, not for you, so that even now, when you're no longer poor, you either don't buy quality items at all or buy them but don't use them. But, you protest, there are people out there who don't have any more than you used to have, you'd feel too guilty, you couldn't possibly, and who knows when the bottom might fall out of the market so you'll need to get every bit of use out of every possession that you possibly can. . . .

Poppycock. Refusing to use your best line of Things doesn't help people who don't have enough, any more than eating your peas helped feed the starving children on the other side of world, as many of us were told. Someone has to use your best Things, and it might as well be you. Start using them, get rid of items that no one would want, and share the rest. While it's true the future is uncertain, what we *do* know is that we have the present—so live it to the fullest today.

93. GATHER SUPPLIES AHEAD OF TIME.

It's Saturday morning and you're about to begin your annual garage clean-out. First you pick up a pile of old rags that are ready to go in the garbage and look around. No garbage bag. You go back in the house and come back out with a bag. Then you begin making piles, and as the piles grow, they begin to merge. It would be better to sort the stuff into boxes, but you don't have any out here. Finally, after going back in again and searching the house from top to bottom, you scrounge up a few, but they're really too small for your purposes. You fill them anyway but, lacking a felt-tipped marker, you don't label them, and consequently after you break for lunch you can't remember which box was for what. And so it goes.

If you don't want your efforts to break down out of frustration, it's important to gather everything you need before you start a project. In the case of de-cluttering this usually includes boxes, trash bags, scissors, markers, cleaning supplies, and new containers. When sorting papers, make sure you also have file boxes or cabinets, hanging folders, file folders, accordion folders in different colors, folder labels, and medium-point black pens or a working label maker with extra cartridges. Before you start your project, get everything out and arrange it neatly so you'll always know where it is while you de-clutter. It's easy for supplies to disappear into clutter piles, never to be seen again, and this will be a lot less likely to happen if you've created a temporary home for each supply item. Be sure to put everything away in its permanent home once you've finished.

When you stop in the middle of an activity to go look for something you need, you're usually in a hurry. You start to balance your checkbook and realize you need last month's statement, then scatter papers from your to-file box all over the desk while you scrounge around for it. Or you go out to plant some flowers and realize you need your gardening gloves, then make a mess in the tool shed trying to find them. Instead of living this way, try for one day to get out everything you need ahead of time when you start each new activity, then put everything away when you're finished. Doesn't this feel better? Make this kind of mindfulness a part of living more clutter-free every day.

94. LEAVE IT NEATER THAN YOU FOUND IT.

In the classic humorous memoir *Cheaper by the Dozen*, Frank B. Gilbreth Jr. and Ernestine Gilbreth Carey, two of the twelve children of the motion-study pioneer Frank Bunker Gilbreth, describe their father's approach to cleaning up after a family picnic at a public campground. Instead of simply having the children clean up the messes they'd made themselves, Dad demanded that they scour the whole picnic ground for trash, regardless of vintage or source, whiskey bottles and all. Clearly his rule was "Leave it neater than you found it." Obviously this man was ahead of his time in teaching his children to do their bit for the environment.

While I'm not suggesting that you routinely pick up after everyone else in your own home, habitually leaving each room a little neater than it was when you entered is more likely to free your life of clutter than not doing so. It doesn't mean you have to clean the room from top to bottom. All you need to do is put away anything you took out and then make three or four more moves in the direction of order. If it's your office, file a few papers. If it's your kitchen, take a few dishes out of the dish drainer or put a pitcher up on a shelf that's been sitting out. If it's your bedroom, fold a blanket that's hanging over a chair.

If you have children, this is a wonderful habit to teach them. Children are natural imitators, and if they see you neatening up each room a little before you leave it, soon they'll be doing it too.

95. SHED SOME LIGHT ON THE SUBJECT.

Clutter, like cockroaches, lurks in dark corners. It's hard to get organized if you can't see your stuff, and it's easier to ignore clutter when the lights are low. Alphabetizing books, writing labels, or sorting clothes by color are all more difficult under poor lighting. Also, in the winter months, many people suffer from seasonal affective disorder (SAD), a condition caused by insufficient sunlight that makes you feel sluggish and sleepy and let Things pile up instead of putting them away. Good lighting, then, is a prerequisite to living more clutter-free.

Take a tour of your home and consider the lighting in each room. Make sure that you have especially good lighting near every reading chair and over desks, the kitchen sink, and other work areas. Any room that doesn't already have a good, bright ceiling light will need something more than just individual table lamps for adequate lighting. I love halogen lamps, which flood whole rooms with light, though you need to be careful not to let them overheat. Never leave the house with a halogen light turned on.

Fluorescent bulbs light up offices, workshops, kitchens, and laundry rooms, but the light they make is harsher than that of halogen lamps, and they buzz when bulbs start burning out. If you suffer from SAD, special high-intensity lights are available. Use these for an hour or so every morning before the sun comes up and you might experience a big boost in your energy level, and help with winter binging as well.

While it's important to conserve electricity by turning lights off when you leave a room, don't deny yourself the lighting you need to be mentally and emotionally healthy during the winter months. Your increased productivity will be well worth the personal and public costs of a few extra watts.

96. SET UP RECYCLE
STATIONS.

Every community has its own list of recyclables and different ways of collecting them. Some pick up and sort nearly everything; others require inhabitants to sort and prepare recyclables themselves; still others will only recycle materials that people bring to a recycling center. To maximize your participation in your community's recycling system, make it as easy as possible for you and your family to collect recyclables in your home. This means setting up recycle stations in convenient locations.

Ideally, you'll set up recycle stations for different materials near the points where you most often encounter them. Place a paper-recycle box in your office. Put containers for cans, glass, and cardboard boxes in the kitchen and a container for newspapers in or at least near the livingroom, if that's where you typically read them. You may want a second container for paper near where you sort the mail. Make a bag for rags where you sew if your community collects fabric; a box for old motor oil bottles in the garage; a plastic bag for used batteries where you keep the new ones. Where you set up other recycle stations will depend on what materials your community collects and where you typically encounter them.

One reason people have difficulty getting rid of Things is environmental conscientiousness. If throwing recyclables in the trash makes you feel guilty—as it should—but organizing them for recycling seems overwhelming, you end up caught in a nasty conflict between guilt and incapacitating overwhelm. Setting up a system of recycling stations releases you from this conflict so that recyclables begin flowing out of your space and into the community's recycling system, reducing your clutter piles.

Along with setting up recycle stations, establish a routine for emptying them. If your community does a curbside pickup, you'll need to take recyclables—probably along with regular trash—out to the curb on the proper day. This is not always easy for everyone, resulting in all sorts of scantily clad people racing out of their houses when the pickup morning arrives. To avoid such crises, put a reminder in your planner or PDA the day *before* the pickup and/or set a reminder alarm to go off in the evening. If you have to take recyclables to a station yourself, schedule this at least once a month and stick to your appointment.

Children are often great sorters and carriers and can be genuinely helpful with recycling. (Don't, however, allow little ones to sort cans and glass unsupervised.) Their participation can both save you work and teach them good recycling habits.

97. LAY THINGS OUT THE NIGHT BEFORE.

If you're not an early riser and tend to create clutter in the morning by racing around, cultivate the habit of laying things out the night before. This can feel wonderful.

Try it. Tonight before you go to bed, think about what tasks you'll need to do in the morning and lay out everything you can that these tasks require. Set the breakfast table and do as much advance preparation as possible for the meal. Fill the coffee maker, slice the coffee cake, pour out cereal. Then make your lunch and put it in the refrigerator. Pack your knapsack or briefcase with everything you'll need to take to work or school in the morning. Hang the clothes you'll be wearing over a chair and arrange tomorrow's toiletries next to the sink. Lay out childrens' clothes, bookbags, allowances, and signed permission slips. Get the dog's leash out, as well as pet foods and medications. Do whatever you can ahead of time.

Then get up and glide through your morning. Since you won't have to turn the house upside down looking for your son's arithmetic book or that check you have to take to the bank, you should have plenty of time to make your bed, hang up your clothes, do the breakfast dishes, and maybe even have a few spare minutes to spend however you like before you leave for work or start your usual chores. Doesn't this feel great?

Believe it or not, there are people who live this way all the time.

98. AM I COMFORTABLE?

A major obstacle to clutter-free living is physical discomfort. Often, when people feel uncomfortable working on a clutter-reducing project, instead of acknowledging their discomfort and solving the problem, they make an excuse and give up. Therefore, when decluttering it's important to keep asking yourself whether or not you're comfortable, and if you're uncomfortable, *how* are you uncomfortable?

Air is the first thing to consider. Is it too hot or too cold in the room where you're working? If so, do you need to adjust the thermostat, turn on the air conditioner or fan, open a window, or change your clothes? Is a draft shooting air on you so you need to close a vent or move? What about the quality of the air? Are you starting to cough and sneeze? If so, you may have a dust or mold allergy that needs to be addressed. You may need to wear a face mask, get medical treatment, or buy an air purifier. Is there a bad smell in the air? Maybe you need to open the windows, scrub out an area, or use an air freshener.

Along with air, consider how your joints and muscles feel. Are you stooping over papers to be filed in a bottom drawer until your back begins to hurt? Maybe you should file the papers in a box on a table first before quickly refiling them in the proper drawer. You may also need to rethink your system, so that the least important papers are kept in the least user-friendly locations. Is the box you've filled with books too heavy for you to carry out to the car so you need to break it up into smaller loads? Are your kitchen counters perpetually cluttered with items that belong on shelves too high or too low for you to easily reach? A good, solid stepladder can help with the high places, and children's help and a clean floor can help with the low ones.

And what about tactile sensations? Have you been putting off dealing with something sticky or slimy or prickly or splintery? Rubber gloves and outdoor work gloves can make it easier. Are you afraid of insects you'll meet when you work in a basement or out of doors? Arm yourself with a good fly swatter.

Even if the discomfort associated with a particular task is a problem for which there's no solution, you'll be more likely to stick with the job if you can name the discomfort to yourself and take the time to problem-solve about possible remedies.

99. HOW MUCH NOISE DO I NEED?

Chances are you know someone who's a stimulation seeker. He or she craves loud music, flashing lights, greasy food, and good times, and may obliviously irritate others by talking loudly on a cell phone in a restaurant. If you're sensitive yourself, being around a person like this can become torture after a while. Such an individual's home and workplace may be both loudly decorated and highly cluttered to produce the maximum amount of stimulation at all times.

Also among your friends and acquaintances may be someone who's stimulation avoidant or hypersensitive. This person hates going to superstores because of the bright lights and noise, prefers classical or easy-listening music, wears all-cotton clothes, eats only natural or gourmet food, and has a living room with white walls and carpeting and hardly anything in it. If you're a stimulation seeker, being with a person like this can be incredibly boring.

Neither of these types is better than the other, they're simply different. Each brain is wired to handle incoming sensations differently, and some brains are wired to take in sensations at a lower frequency than others, like some radios receive AM and others receive FM transmissions. Stimulation threshold has nothing to do with intelligence; you can be smart and either hypersensitive or undersensitive to stimuli. Not everyone, of course, falls at one extreme or the other on the stimulation continuum. Many people fall somewhere in between.

Recognizing how much stimulation you like in your life can help you live more clutter-free. If you're stimulation avoidant, clutter might mean something different for you than if you're a stimulation seeker. If you're hypersensitive, you might feel that you're living in a mess with even a small amount of disorder, one that stimulation seekers wouldn't even notice. This can lead to your spending excessive time and energy perfecting what is already nearly perfect, time and energy that you could better use another way. In that case, you might want to raise your tolerance for clutter by allowing a little more chaos into your life than you're currently comfortable with. This will allow you to start living instead of cleaning all the time.

If you're a stimulation seeker, on the other hand, you might create high levels of clutter to provide the stimulation you need. At the same time, you might hate not being able to find Things and be embarrassed to invite friends over. If that's the case, try to find other ways of creating visual and emotional stimulation. Put up lots of pictures, the more vivid and ornate the better. Choose upholstered furniture with printed fabrics and sprinkle lots of knickknacks around. Buy some lava lamps, play as much loud music as your neighbors will tolerate, use furry fabrics, and burn incense.

In striving to reduce clutter, take your stimulation threshold into account. Sensation seekers might quickly become bored when sorting papers and need to add loud music and good company to make the task bearable, while a grungy, physical job such as cleaning out a basement is more appealing. Hypersensitive types, on the other hand, might need to close the door to keep from being distracted from a task and pay someone else to clean out their smelly garage or musty attic.

Wherever you are on this spectrum, the key, as in all things, is to *know thyself,* and take what you know into account when you design your activities, surroundings, goals, and game plan.

100. CHART YOUR PROGRESS AT LIVING CLUTTER-FREE.

While you're getting rid of a backlog of clutter from years past, it's easy to monitor your progress. You can simply watch the piles shrink day by day. Once the big clutter is gone, however, it becomes more difficult to see where you're going and where you've been. One day a little clutter piles up, the next day it goes away, the day after that a little piles up again, and so forth, day after day. It's like weighing yourself when you're close to your ideal weight. To stay motivated during the post-de-cluttering phase, you need a special method of following your progress that allows you to recognize overall trends rather than little ups and downs.

One such method is to keep a daily journal in which you scribble just a few lines describing your daily clutter issues and the feelings you have about them: "Up early, made bed, de-cluttered living room, still didn't hang up work clothes. Why can't I make myself? I'm sooo frustrated!" As you read back through such entries, you'll begin to see patterns. This will allow you to monitor progress, not just in your environment but in your thoughts and feelings as well.

For the external, visible piece, pictures can do a lot more than words. Tour your house with your camera once a month for a year. When you get the pictures, put dates on them and sort them by room. Again, patterns will emerge, and you'll see that, despite small-scale ups and downs, the clutter *is* diminishing.

Finally, if you like numbers, walk around once a month and rate each room for clutter on a scale from 0 to 10 (0 = no clutter at all; 10 = totally packed). Average your findings and plot them on a graph. As you continue to work on living clutter-free, the line on the graph may dip at times, but hopefully the overall trend will be upward.

Such strategies will help you get used to your new lifestyle. At some point, you won't need them anymore. By then, if all goes well, you won't be wasting hours looking for Things you can't find. You'll be able to sit down without moving anything. You'll enjoy spending time in your space and entertaining family and friends. You'll glide more smoothly through your days and nights, have more time and energy available for the people and activities you care about, and be able to focus on new goals. You'll be living clutter-free every day.

RESOURCES FOR HELP WITH ORGANIZING

Cindy Glovinsky's Web site:
www.freshstartorganizing.com

This Web site contains information about Cindy's organizing business, Fresh Start Organizing, as well as about how to order this book and Cindy's other book, *Making Peace with the Things in Your Life.*

ORGANIZATIONS:

National Association of Professional Organizers (NAPO)
35 Technology Parkway South, Suite 150
Norcross, GA 30092
770-325-3440 (information and referral line)
770-263-8825 (fax)
www.napo.net

Gives referrals for professional organizers.

National Study Group on Chronic Disorganization
P.O. Box 1990
Elk Grove, CA 95759
916-962-6227
www.nsgcd.org

Gives referrals for professional organizers specializing in chronic disorganization.

BIBLIOGRAPHY

Barkley, Russell. *Taking Charge of ADHD,* New York: The Guilford Press, 1995.

Barnes, Emilie. *The 15 Minute Organizer.* Eugene, Ore.: Harvest House Press, 1991.

Csikzentmihalyi, Mihaly. *Flow: The Psychology of Optimal Experience.* New York: HarperPerennial, 1990.

Culp, Stephanie. *How to Conquer Clutter.* Cincinnati, Ohio: Writer's Digest, 1990.

Felton Sandra. *The Messies Superguide.* Grand Rapids, Mich.: Fleming H. Revell, 1987.

Gilbreth, Frank B., and Ernestine Gilbreth Carey. *Cheaper by the Dozen.* New York: Thomas Y. Crowell, 1948.

Glovinsky, Cindy. *Making Peace with the Things in Your Life.* New York: St. Martin's Press, 2002.

Katherine, Anne. *Where to Draw the Line.* New York: Simon & Schuster, 2000.

Klauser, Henriette. *Write it Down, Make it Happen.* New York: Scribner, 2000.

Kolberg, Judith, and Kathleen Nadeau. *ADD-Friendly Ways to Organize Your Life.* New York: Brunner-Routledge, 2002.

Kolberg, Judith. *Conquering Chronic Disorganization.* Decatur, Ga.: Squall Press, 1999.

Lehmkuhl, Dorothy, and Dolores Cotter Lamping. *Organizing for the Creative Person.* New York: Crown Publishers, 1993.

MacDonald, Betty. *Mrs. Piggle-Wiggle.* New York: HarperCollins, 1947.

Maslow, Abraham. *Motivation and Personality.* New York: Harper & Brothers, 1954.

Moore, Thomas. *Care of the Soul.* New York: HarperCollins, 1992.

Morgenstern, Julie. *Organizing from the Inside Out.* New York: Henry Holt, 1998.

Passoff, Michelle. *Lighten Up! Free Yourself from Clutter.* New York: HarperCollins, 1998.

Piaget, Jean. *The Construction of Reality in the Child.* New York: Ballantine Books, 1954.

Ratey, John. *A User's Guide to the Brain.* New York: Pantheon Books, 2001.

Smallin, Donna. *Organizing Plain & Simple.* North Adams, Mass.: Storey Publishing, 2002.

Schechter, Harriet. *Let Go of Clutter.* New York: McGraw-Hill, 2001.

Solden, Sari. *Women with Attention Deficit Disorder.* Grass Valley, Calif.: Underwood Books, 1995.

Waddill, Kathy. *The Organizing Sourcebook.* New York: McGraw-Hill, 2001.

Wickham, Zenita. "Purge." *Balance,* Fall 2002.

Winston, Stephanie. *Best Organizing Tips.* New York: Fireside, 1995.

Young, Pam, and Peggy Jones. *Sidetracked Home Executives.* New York: Warner Books, 2001.